GOOD · OLD · DAYS®
Our Favorite
pets™

Edited by Ken and Janice Tate

HOUSE of
WHITE
BIRCHES
PUBLISHERS
SINCE 1947

Our Favorite Pets™

Editors: Ken and Janice Tate
Managing Editor: Barb Sprunger
Editorial Assistant: Sara Meyer
Copy Supervisor: Michelle Beck
Copy Editors: Läna Schurb, Judy Weatherford

Publishing Services Director: Brenda Gallmeyer
Art Director: Brad Snow
Assistant Art Director: Nick Pierce
Graphic Arts Supervisor: Ronda Bechinski
Production Artists: Nicole Gage, Janice Tate
Production Assistants: Marj Morgan, Jessica Tate
Photography: Tammy Christian, Matt Owen
Photo Stylist: Tammy Steiner

Printed in China
First Printing: 2008
Library of Congress Number: 2007937751
ISBN: 978-1-59217-213-9

Good Old Days Customer Service: (800) 829-5865

We would like to thank the following for the art prints used in this book.
For fine-art prints and more information on the artists featured in *Our Favorite Pets* contact:
Curtis Publishing, Indianapolis, IN 46202, (317) 633-2070, All rights reserved. www.curtispublishing.com
Jim Daly, P.O. Box 25146, Eugene, OR 97402, www.jimdalyart.com
Norman Rockwell Family Trust, Antrim, NH 03440, (603) 588-3512
Wild Wings Inc., Lake City, MN 55041 (800) 445-4833, www.wildwings.com

1 2 3 4 5 6 7 8 9

Dear Friends of the Good Old Days,

It's a good thing I wasn't allergic to animals back when I was a youngster. By the time I reached adolescence, our little home in the Ozark Mountains of southern Missouri was the equivalent of a domesticated zoo.

Dogs, cats, incubating chicks, ducks, piglets and the occasional garter snake (at least until Mama found out about it)—all found their way at one time or another inside our walls.

The animal kingdom was even more diverse outside those walls. Horses, cattle, pigs and fowl of every feathered description populated our little farm. And the woods at the perimeter provided the occasional orphaned rabbit, raccoon, squirrel or fawn to nurture.

I considered every one of them my friend, my confidant, my pet.

It would be pretty hard for me to pick my favorite pet from the Good Old Days. My earliest recollection of any animal specifically considered a pet was Grandma Stamps' woolly shepherd-collie Poochie. (Not a very original name, I know, but we were pretty simplistic when it came to naming our pets.) Grandma lived a short walk from our house; she and Poochie were both babysitters for me as oft as I could sneak away. Poochie was old in my earliest memory of him, and he lived to an ancient age, nearly until my 13th birthday.

Then there was Blackie, the black terrier who became our first indoor pet. Like a lot of my animal friends, Blackie just showed up at our door and became part of the family. He slept with my brother and me. He was my companion on real-life hunting trips, not to mention the imaginary journeys that took me pirating on the ocean, exploring in South America or big-game safaris in

Africa. We ran together, swam together, camped together. We even ate together when Mama wasn't looking!

Blackie lived with us over a decade until one day he left for his morning walk and never showed up again, leaving us as mysteriously as he arrived. It took a couple of days, but when the reality of his departure sank in, I was inconsolable. Life without him was seemingly impossible.

I guess that is what pets have always done best. They fill our young lives with laughter and pain, with tears of joy and tears of sorrow. Animals give us some of our most tender moments, but they also help teach us the harsh realities of life.

Recently my dear wife, Janice, and I asked the readers of *Good Old Days* magazine to share stories of their own animal friends. That was the genesis of this special book. So find a comfortable chair, relax and go back with us as we remember the Good Old Days and our favorite pets.

❦ Contents ❦

On the Wild Side • 100

Farm Friends • 128

A Kid's Best Friend

Chapter One

Friskie was the best friend a kid could ever hope for back in the Good Old Days. My part-shepherd, part-collie companion showed up in our front yard when I was about 9 years old. I guess he really wasn't "my" dog—or even "our" dog. Friskie was an independent spirit who just chose to join his life to ours for the next 12 or 13 years.

I guess some would question giving "best friend" status to an animal, but if so they have not weighed the meaning of friendship.

I would place Friskie's friendship on the same level as any of my adolescent companions. His love and devotion to me was, in fact, even greater than most.

I am reminded of the words of George Graham Vest, a U.S. Senator from my home state of Missouri. In 1855, Vest was the attorney for a man who was suing another for killing his dog, Old Drum. He won the case largely on his summation to the jury:

"The one absolutely unselfish friend that man can have in this selfish world, the one that never deserts him, the one that never proves ungrateful or treacherous is his dog. A man's dog stands by him in prosperity and in poverty, in health and in sickness. … When all other friends desert, he remains. When riches take wings, and reputation falls to pieces, he is as constant in his love as the sun in its journey through the heavens.

"If fortune drives the master forth, an outcast in the world, friendless and homeless, the faithful dog asks no higher privilege than that of accompanying him, to guard him against danger, to fight against his enemies. And when the last scene of all comes, and death takes his master in its embrace and his body is laid away in the cold ground, no matter if all other friends pursue their way, there by the graveside will the noble dog be found, his head between his paws, his eyes sad, but open in alert watchfulness, faithful and true even in death."

There was little doubt in my mind that Friskie was my best friend. I spent more time with Friskie than with any of my childhood chums.

"The one absolutely unselfish friend that a man can have … is his dog."

He was always waiting for me at the front screen door when I charged out of it to meet a new day. With the exception of school days, church and mealtimes, we shared the days almost inseparably. He faithfully stayed by my side until I left him by the door in the evening.

I remember the time he valiantly threw himself between me and a copperhead. He killed the snake with a mighty shaking in his powerful jaws—but not before taking a venomous injury to the snout. When the swelling became severe, I feared losing my buddy, but with Mama's help, I nursed him back to health.

I was the only one Friskie would allow to help him when he was hurt. Once, he picked up a thorn that stuck between his pads and showed up at our home limping terribly. I soothed him into letting me examine the paw. Despite Mama's fears that he would snap at me in pain, I extracted the offending sticker. It was the least I could do for my best friend.

The stories in this chapter remember the Good Old Days when a dog was more than just an animal or a pet. He was a member of the extended family, a companion, a confidant and, ultimately, a Kid's Best Friend.

—Ken Tate

Pudgy

By Anthony Curtacci

*I*t was June back in 1957. School had just let out for the long summer vacation. The kids on my street were thinking about two months with nothing to do but enjoy being kids. A few days went by, and then Mom announced that we had a summer job. We'd be going for six weeks to work at a summer camp in the Adirondacks. We'd spend six weeks on a private lake, with all the swimming and fishing I could handle.

The camp had a large mess hall, the director's house and a small cabin. There would be 10 or 12 counselors for about 60 boys who slept in tents. The cabin behind the mess hall was for the kitchen crew, three other boys, myself and, of course, Pudgy.

At this time, Pudgy was 8 or 9 years old. She had been born on the Lairdsville, N.Y., farm belonging to our friend Jerry. She was one of four puppies. Deana, Jerry's daughter, had already named her Bashful, but it was apparent she wasn't, so we changed her name. She didn't seem to mind.

Go home without Pudgy? No way! I hoped to find my dog. I had to!

Her mother and one older brother lived on the farm. It was their job to bring in the cows at milking time. They knew when it was time, and they would take off and quickly round them up and bring them in. They were collie-shepherd mix, and almost all white. Pudgy had some white, too, but she was mostly brown. She was a large, strong, smart dog, and she protected me and went everywhere with me.

Pudgy had a busy day at home. She was up and out early in the morning so she could follow our mailman on his route. She would protect him from the other dogs. At the end of his route, she would walk him home and have lunch with him. If she failed to show, he'd call to inquire if she was OK.

After leaving him, she'd make a stop at the corner market where the butcher would be waiting for her, usually with a large bone, which she'd bring home and chew up in the yard. She also spent hours in the garden with my grandfather. He would stop and pet her, and the pair seemed to understand one another.

Once while we were away for the day, Walt, a close family friend who visited often, came by. Now, Pudgy knew and loved Walt, but even so, when he reached for the doorknob, she gently grabbed his sleeve and stopped him. He laughed to himself and reached several times, and every time the same thing happened.

He thought it was great; obviously she was telling him that nobody was home. He could pet her and rub her ears, but he wasn't allowed to touch the doorknob.

Our days at the camp soon fell into a routine. We'd swim in the afternoon and fish away the evening, at least until the Fourth of July came along. That weekend, the director's brother showed up with some firecrackers. He was showing off for some of the boys and threw some near Pudgy and scared her. She then ran into the woods that surrounded the lake.

I was working in the mess hall at the time, and didn't hear what had happened for some time. Then one of the boys who liked Pudgy a lot came and told me she had run off and hadn't come back. At first I wasn't worried. I thought she was just hiding. After all, she wandered everywhere at home and always came back—but this wasn't Whitesboro.

That evening, I searched the whole area around the lake and called her, but no Pudgy. I didn't sleep much that night, and I was up early—but no Pudgy.

Now I had a knot in my stomach, and I feared for my best pal. I found the camp director and told him I wouldn't be working anymore until I found her—and his brother had better pray that I did.

Starting that day and every day for what seemed like forever, I was up early and into the woods, up and down the roads that surrounded the lake and the area by the stream. At least twice I got lost myself, but I would come across a dirt road that eventually led me out.

I called and called, but there was no answer. I found a couple of dead animals, too. "I can't find Pudgy like this," I thought.

One day, I came across an old, falling-down house. I peeked inside; chairs, pictures and kitchen stuff were still there. It looked like someone had walked away one day and never come back. But still, no Pudgy.

The end of the camp season was coming fast, and this upset me. They would close up camp, and everyone would go home. Go home without Pudgy? No way! I hoped to find my dog. I had to!

But then people started telling me to give up. They said something must have happened to her. They told me to face it, but that just pushed me harder.

I decided to expand my search. I would cross the bridge onto the main road and go up to where there were a few camps. Maybe someone had seen her.

When I knocked at the very first cabin I came to, an elderly couple answered. There was a small pond out behind the cabin and a very old truck in the yard. I told them who I was and asked if they had seen a strange dog around. The lady smiled and said, "Yes. The dog comes here every night and is gone in the morning. We gave her a few crusts of bread, but we knew she must belong to someone." They didn't want her to stay and not find her way back.

I looked all around and called to her, but there was no answer.

Maybe it's not her, I thought. But I told them where to find me and begged them to contact me if she came back again.

That night at suppertime, one of the campers came to find me, yelling, "There's some old guy in an old truck looking for you."

I ran and the old man yelled, "The dog is back!" I grabbed the director and dragged him to his car. Up the road, over the bridge, and up the main road we went. The lady was outside, but she said, "The dog just ran back into the woods."

I ran in the direction she pointed, yelling, "Pudgy! Pudgy! Come on, girl!" Suddenly, out of the thick brush came Pudgy, running full out. She knocked me down and we rolled around in the road in delight. How great was this? Pudgy was very thin after nine days in the woods, but I'd fatten her up quickly. Just two days later, we returned home.

Pudgy lived to be 19, and I was married and had a son before she died. She would lie next to his carriage and defy anyone to come near. We had 19 great years together, except for those nine days in the summer of 1957.

I hope that old couple knew how happy they made me, because now I can remember old Pudgy without that knot in my stomach. And I pray that someday, we'll find each other again! ❖

Zip, the Dog?

By Karen Bowen

When our daughters were ages 2 and 5, Santa brought them a black-and-white mixed-breed puppy that our kindergartner immediately named Zip after the dog in her *My Weekly Reader*.

Zip became devoted to the children and constantly shadowed them during their back-yard play.

Regardless of the activity or game, Zip was in the midst, keeping a sharp eye lest they stray from her designated boundaries. She was as much a part of the gang as the endless neighborhood children who often joined in the fun.

I was not aware of Zip's special status until one afternoon, when I heard our older daughter say to her sister, "Let's play house. I'll be the mother, you can be the kid and we'll *pretend* that Zip is the dog."

And so, for nearly 16 years, we all "pretended" that Zip was a dog.

Well, Zip must have gotten into the spirit of "let's pretend," because one summer, we took her to a children's pet show at a local country fair.

The families were all seated on benches in front of the stage, and as each child's name was called, she walked her dog across and received an award.

All the other dogs sat on the ground at the foot of their child, but not Zip. She sat *on* the bench, giving careful attention to what was happening on stage. No amount of coaxing could convince her to relinquish her seat.

That's when we knew for sure that, at least in her mind, Zip wasn't really a dog. ❖

John's Dog

By Millie Smith

Great-Aunt Rena always started talking the minute we entered her house. She usually started with, "Did I ever tell you about ... ?" and continued with a story out of her past that would catch our interest and keep us there as long as possible.

She was a lonely old lady. One time she asked, "Did I ever tell you about the time I killed your Uncle John's dog?" and before we could answer, she launched into her story:

"Well, I never did care much about dogs anyway, and this was a real sorry-looking mutt. I guess he was part Airedale. Anyway, he was about the size of a Shetland pony. John got the dog for protection and company when he had that gas station in Baldwin, and the dog always stayed right there at the station. He named him Rex.

"John had to close the station and go to work on the night shift at the canning factory during the Depression, so he brought old Rex home and fixed him a bed in the woodshed. I wouldn't have that miserable mutt in the house.

"Every night after John went to work, Rex started to howl, and he kept it up all night. I couldn't get a decent night's sleep. In the morning, when John came home from work, he went directly to the woodshed, patted the dog's head, scratched his ears and talked to him for a while.

"He would come in the house, mumble a greeting to me, and lapse into silence while he ate breakfast. I got to thinking that John liked that dog better than he did me. Made me mad.

"Lately, several neighbors had complained about Rex running through their gardens, and of course, those big feet of his tore up lots of their vegetables. One gardener shot him with a BB gun. Must have stung a bit, because I heard him *yip-yipping* all the way home. But it didn't stop him from galloping through the same garden the next day. I was always having to deal with neighbors' complaints.

"One day, I noticed that Rex seemed sick. He just lay on that old blanket in the shed and wouldn't eat. But still, after a week of acting puny, he had strength enough to howl at night.

"That night, after John had gone to work, I decided what to do. I made up my mind to kill that dog. He was old and sick and really should be put out of his misery, I told myself. So I took a handful of hamburger and worked a whole bottle of aspirin into it, until I had a nice firm ball.

After a week of acting puny, he had strength enough to howl at night.

"*That'll fix him*, I thought as I opened the shed door and tossed the meat in. Then I went in the house and had the best night's sleep I'd had in a long time. There was no dog howling.

"The first thing I thought of when I woke up was *What will John say when he finds out I killed his dog?* As I fixed breakfast, I got more and more nervous about it, wondering just how mad John would be. Then, looking out the window, I saw John driving in and around to the back where the shed was. I knew I was in for big trouble.

"Now the door opened, and John said, 'What did you do to my dog?' I couldn't even turn to look at him. I just kept stirring the oatmeal. When he asked a second time, I said, 'Not a thing. Is something wrong?'

"'That's the funniest thing,' John replied. 'Last night, when I left for work, old Rex just lay there like he was darn near dead. This morning when I opened the shed door, he was out of there like a shot and took off across the field at full speed. He hasn't had that much energy in years.'

"All I could think to say was, 'It's a miracle!'"

When we asked Auntie what had become of Rex, she said through clenched teeth, "He lived for several more years. Outlived John." ❖

Brutus

By Jay T. Cloud

Cracking corn for the chickens was one of my chores on the farm. On my way to the corncrib, I saw one of our more distant neighbors walking down a dirt road to the river. At the same instant, he saw me and called me over. On the way, I noticed he had a sack slung over his shoulder.

"Want a pup, son? No one else seems to want the little fellow."

"Yes sir, you bet I do!" I was really excited.

I knew now what was in the sack, and also what the trip to the river meant.

He sat the sack down. There was only one pup in it, the runt. As soon as I saw the dog, my estimation of the man went up. He had been trying to give him away for some time. He did not want to drown that pup.

By risking the wrath of my father, I could save the perky little mutt. Taking my prize, I raced back to the house to tell my mother. She was my first and best line of defense when my father found out what had happened.

> *"I'll take care of him," I promised with all the sincerity I could muster.*

"You should have asked," she said sternly, but her blue eyes were smiling.

"I'll take care of him," I promised with all the sincerity I could muster. My sister, who was into Roman history at the time, decided Brutus was a good name for him.

After an initial frown, my father seemed to accept the situation. I suspect my mother had talked to him. He pronounced the dog a mongrel, with a strong strain of shepherd.

Brutus grew rapidly, and we became inseparable. As he became a full-grown dog, he lived up to my father's analysis, showing an affinity for the farm stock. Dad trained him to herd the stock in from the pasture. The cows were simple, and he moved them in slowly. The horses were an entirely different situation. A sorrel stallion named Rube showed no fear of anything. Even my father was cautious when dealing with that horse.

Rube and Brutus absolutely hated each other. When Brutus started to bring the horses in, the stallion refused to move. The dog would nip the stud's heels. Knowing he could not outrun the instant kick that followed, the dog would flatten himself to the ground. The kick would go over Brutus, and when the horse's hoof returned to the ground, the dog would nip him again. This skirmish continued all the way to the barn.

Facing page: *Boy and Dog in Nature* by Eugene Iverd © 1932 SEPS: Licensed by Curtis Publishing

I fed Rube apples and sugar cubes, making him my pet. Often he came to the fence near the house and whinnied for his treats. If Brutus was with me—and he always was—the stallion would snort, toss his head and paw the ground.

The dog reacted with complete disdain. He paid no attention to the stud unless he had been sent to bring him to the barn.

Brutus was a dog of many talents. I taught him to run rabbits. Note the difference between "run" and "chase." If the dog does not press the rabbit too hard, the rabbit will run in a large circle, returning just about to the place where he was jumped. The rabbit unfolds his bag of tricks as he goes, doubling back and going through thick briar patches. Brutus yelped with pain when the briars scratched his ears.

Usually I would call the dog off, unless rabbits were wreaking havoc in our garden. In such a case, rabbit was apt to be on the dinner menu.

Another job Brutus and I had was to keep woodchucks out of the pasture field. A stream ran through the pasture, and nearby was an excellent place for a groundhog to dig a hole. The trouble was, if livestock stepped in the hole, a broken leg could result.

We hunted for their dens, and when we found one, I would pour water into the hole until the woodchuck was forced out. Brutus would chase him to a thicket or a dense briar patch

where the livestock were not apt to graze, and I would fill the hole with stones from the creek.

If the occupant proved recalcitrant or hostile, I would take a rifle along, and he would likely end up on the dinner table. Groundhog is very good when properly prepared.

One morning on the way to fill the watering trough, I spotted a copperhead snake about 10 feet from the foundation of the barn. I quietly went to the toolshed and armed myself with a goosenecked hoe. A hoe is a deadly weapon to use against any snake. I knew that if I attacked,

Photo by Russell Lee, August 1942, courtesy the FSA-OWI Collection, Library of Congress

Brutus would attack, and I was afraid that in the ensuing melee, one or both of us could be bitten. I didn't want to lose my dog, and I didn't want the snake to escape into a crevice in the barn foundation.

The main idea was to get Brutus out of the picture. When a dog attacks a snake, he shakes it violently and tries to throw it beyond striking range. There is no way of telling which way the snake will go.

After extracting a solemn promise of good treatment, I gave him to the stockman.

I was in a quandary. Then my mother came to the other side of the barn with a pail of milk.

"Mom, will you call Brutus?" I asked in a muted voice.

"Why, Honey?" It was a perfectly logical question.

"Please, Mom, just call Brutus." She must have heard the desperation in my voice.

"Come here, Brutus," she called. Brutus trotted over, wagging from the ears back, and followed her toward the house.

I slowly approached the snake. It saw me at once and did not retreat, but coiled in a striking position. A snake does not know that a hoe is not part of a human being. I teased the copperhead into a strike at the hoe. Once the snake was stretched out, I dispatched it with three quick blows.

Brutus must have heard the commotion. He came racing to the scene. I grabbed him by the collar and locked him in the toolshed over his howls of protest. Then I went over the area carefully to make sure the copperhead didn't have a mate nearby.

After the snake's burial, Brutus was released. He went over the scene in detail and, satisfied, reared up on me to show I was forgiven for locking him in the toolshed.

We returned to the house to find my parents in a deep discussion about whether to leave the farm and move to the edge of town for an easier life. I was flattered that they wanted my opinion. I was all for the move. Jobs were scarce, but I was old enough to enlist in the military if my parents signed for me. I selected the Marine Corps. The move was accomplished, and I entered the military service.

The only one left out was Brutus. He roamed the neighborhood, a friendly dog, but soon the neighbors were complaining about his trespassing. To tie such a dog was unthinkable.

A cattleman out in the country had seen him work and wanted to buy him. Selling my old companion was not to be considered, but after extracting a solemn promise of good treatment, I gave him to the stockman.

I did not go to see Brutus at his new home. In my opinion, it was not in the best interests of either of us. I did call the new owner, and he assured me the dog was busy, healthy, happy and had the freedom of the farm. He was home again. I wonder if Brutus remembers me. I know I shall never forget him. ❖

Snowball Goes to School

By Lucille Hawk

I am 68 years old, and these events happened when I was in the fifth through the eighth grades of school.

My cousin had a very cute little puppy that I loved very much. I went by his house on the way to and from school, and every day, I begged my cousin to give me the puppy. He finally got tired of me and gave her to me.

I named her Snowball. As soon as she got big enough, she walked to school with me every day. She slept under my desk until recess or lunch, and then she went out to play when I did. The only trouble Snowball ever got into was for eating a child's lunch and damaging another student's English book. My parents had to pay for the book.

Snowball attended school more than some of the pupils did. She was the greatest pet I ever had. ❖

Sharing A Name With My Dog

By Ginger K. Nelson

My dog named me when she came into my life in 1950 when I was 11 years old. I didn't name the 3-year-old wirehaired fox terrier because she already had a name registered with the American Kennel Club—Pretty Ginger Kay. I already had a name, also; mine was Louise Ann Kirk—Louise after my mother and her aunt Louisa, and Ann after her sister, Annie, and her mother, Anna.

Although a great deal of family history was wrapped in my given name, the notion of changing it was nothing new. Throughout my childhood, I was always inventing new designations for myself—Daphne and Mikey, to recall a couple. But the day the dog Ginger became mine, I decided on the final and lasting way to address me—Ginger. Eventually my family got used to it.

At first, it was embarrassing to explain the true origin of my nickname, so instead, I cited a current play on Broadway, *Time Out for Ginger*. My Aunt Butchie took me to see it, as we lived nearby in Wood-Ridge, N.J., a mere half-hour bus ride from New York City.

My teacher didn't know about my new name, so I used it to sign the notes I passed in school. All my friends had dogs, and they all followed suit, thinking it would fool our teacher. She was unaware of who was really behind the signatures of Scotty, Rusty and Ginger—at least we thought so. As it turned out, she recognized our handwriting, so she knew exactly who had written the notes.

That Broadway play moved on. I didn't. As you might

Ginger and Ginger in 1950.

have guessed, I was focused on nicknames in those years. Today's young people may be content with their names, but my passion to call everybody by a nickname continued for half a decade.

Ginger (the dog) inspired me in many ways. Like most preteens who have pets, I learned to meet her basic needs. It was a pleasure to pour the food into her bowl and watch that furry tail wag in response. She loved going for walks with me. She also filled my need for companionship. I had many friends but no siblings, but as long as I had Ginger, I always had someone to cuddle with and play with. And I had something not many others had: a pet who shared my name.

Although it isn't easy to teach tricks to a 3-year-old dog, I did manage "shake your paw," but little else. Unfortunately, she never learned to stop her one bad habit. Whenever the telephone or doorbell rang, Ginger barked painfully until it was silent. The ringing hurt her ears, and she simply wanted the noise to end.

Whenever I arrived home, she would bark a few friendly words of greeting. Whenever I climbed into bed, she knew she was welcome to join me.

Ginger was there for those tumultuous years when I went from being a preteen to a teen trying to "find myself." Did she ever tire of hearing those confidences about which cute boy had spoken to me? Which teacher had embarrassed or annoyed me? Which friend had eaten lunch at my table at school? Did she ever get jealous when Joanne spent the night, when Priscilla enjoyed my company after school or when Cathy invited me to play stickball in the empty playground on Saturdays? Although some of the adults in my life thought I assigned too many human qualities to Ginger, my friends who were pet lovers understood that my dog was another person in my life.

No one was surprised that I cried when I learned that Ginger had been put to sleep after being diagnosed with cancer. My mom had taken her to the vet while I was busy learning to conjugate Latin verbs and solve the *X* in algebra. "I didn't even have a chance to say goodbye!" I wailed.

My family decided to surprise me with a new dog. They hoped it would be just the ticket

Tippy

By Winnie Schuetz

Tippy was my only dog during my growing-up years. One day, my daddy came home with a tiny puppy nestled in his shirt pocket. It was a fuzzy white puppy, part Spitz and part poodle.

Tippy was my faithful pal. I told him all my troubles. Mom said, "No dogs in the house." Daddy was a carpenter, and he built Tippy a deluxe house. When I got in a jam with Mom, I would crawl into the doghouse with Tippy and cry and tell him my woes.

Tippy lived to be 21 years old. He grew to love my husband Lewis, and when he was hurt or sick, he let Lewis tend him like a nurse. When Tippy died, we buried him out on the farm where we lived.

Tippy meant a lot to me, perhaps because I was sometimes lonely as an only child. I have never forgotten him all these years. ❖

to restore a back-to-normal Ginger (the person) instead of the Ginger who had been drooping around the house for several weeks.

Although I tried to seem grateful, the new dog became my mom's responsibility. She didn't really have the time to care for him, as she was a single mother earning a living, keeping house and making sure her daughter obeyed the rules. When Mom offered to give the dog away, I concurred that it would be best for everyone. We found a good home for him and closed our door to pets.

As an adult, I'm often asked whether my name is really Virginia. Now I'm not embarrassed to explain, "No, I called myself after my dog." Others assume that my red hair gave birth to my name. "No," I reply, "I called myself after my dog."

Few people—except others who have lost their beloved pets—can understand that no matter how many years have passed, I still think of Pretty Ginger Kay whenever anyone addresses me. People have called me Ginger for the past 50-plus years, and as you see by my byline, I also use it as my pen name. ❖

The Dog Who Adopted My Family

By Julia Rankin

*I*t was a cold night when Papa came home late for supper when we first saw Billy. The *flip-flop* of old Jim's feet and the squeak of the wagon sent three small children rushing out onto the back porch. When Papa came into the light of the kitchen window, they saw a big black-and-white dog following him. Instead of greeting Papa with his usual bear hug, little Kirk threw his arms around the dog and patted his wet fur, saying, "My doggie, my doggie." The dog licked the tiny hands. It seemed to be love at first sight.

When Amy patted the dog, Kirk said jealously, "He's *my* doggie." Kathy's welcome was cordial, too.

Mama hurried from the kitchen, saw the dog and protested, "He's too big and dirty. He might bite the children."

"Oh, no," Papa disagreed. "See how gentle he is?"

"Can we keep him?" Amy asked eagerly.

A big tear rolled down Kirk's cheek. The dog tenderly licked it away.

"He's my doggie!" Kirk declared. "Mine—and he's not a dog; he's a *people*."

"Now see what you've done, bringing that dog home!"

"I didn't bring him. He followed me," Papa defended. "He'd been hanging around the store all day…"

"You gave him your lunch," Mama interrupted.

"Well, I got along on cheese and crackers."

"We must keep him," Kathy said firmly.

"If no one claims him, we'll talk about it later," Papa promised.

"He's so big," Mama protested weakly.

"He'd be a protection for the children."

"Ye-s-s?"

"Then we'll leave it until tomorrow—unless …"

"Then come in out of the cold and eat supper," Mama called.

The next morning, when Papa was ready to go to work, three little children stood in a row. In front of them, as if on guard, stood the dog.

"Well, dog, are you going with me?" Papa asked.

The dog took one step forward, but at the sound of a little sob, he turned his head. A big tear rolled down Kirk's cheek. The dog tenderly licked it away.

"There's your answer," Papa said. Mama nodded surrender.

"Get up, Old Jim. It's time for us to go to work."

The next night, Kathy reminded the family that our new member didn't have a name. "Let's call him Rascal."

"No," Kirk objected. "He is not a rascal. His name is Billy 'cause I said so."

Children do grow older, and when Amy was in her teens, she asked me to show her how to make the "dream pie" I had learned to make in cooking class. We made one. It was good, and afterward, Amy made one all by herself. It was to be our dessert that night.

Before she cut it, she turned it this way and that, admiring its perfection. Suddenly it slipped from her hands and landed on the floor, upside-down. Her face was a map of horrified surprise and dismay. She stared at it for a moment, then said, "I'm not going to clean it up."

I wondered how she would get by with that. She went to the door and called Billy. When he came in, she pointed to the smashed pie and said, "Eat." He did, and he licked the floor clean.

"See, Billy liked it, and he cleaned the floor, too."

Mama didn't object to Billy's method of floor cleaning, but the next morning, that spot smelled like soap and water.

Billy took his job of protecting us seriously—sometimes *too* seriously, even for Kirk. While I was washing dishes, Kirk oozed into the kitchen and whispered, "Keep Billy from following me."

"Why? I don't like to be Billy's jailer."

"The boys are going to play ball."

"Well, take Billy along. He likes to play ball, too."

"But we can't play when he's around! He runs away with the ball!"

Then there was the time I was watching a summer shower coming over the hills. At first it was far off, but then it drew closer—and then something was pulling the hem of my skirt. It was Billy, with anxious eyes. He ran toward the house and looked back to see if I was following. He seemed to think I didn't have enough sense to come in out of the rain.

It was useless to protest, so I followed meekly. I sat on the porch, with Billy lying at my feet—between me and the porch steps.

When Kirk was a student in military college, his visits home were a joy to him and to Billy. All the students wore uniforms, much like soldiers wore. Billy didn't know this, and that was his undoing.

It happened when Kathy's friend from an Army camp came to visit her. Charles was a diplomatic person, so he helped Papa feed the pigs. While they were standing by the fence, watching the pigs eat, Billy came home. From a distance, he saw Papa and a uniform. Filled with joy that his beloved Kirk was home, he bounded over and jumped on the shoulders of the uniform. Both he and Charles fell against the fence and tumbled down.

When they got themselves unscrambled, they stared at each other. Billy saw his mistake—it was not his beloved Kirk, but a stranger. With head and tail down, he fled to a dark corner under the back porch. He refused to eat or come out until Charles's visit was over.

Years later, I told Amy about the uniform mix-up. She softly sniffed and gently wiped her eyes and said, "I can cry for Billy now. He was so disappointed."

Our family had many happy years with Billy, and many heartbreaking ones, too. When Mama died, he shared our grief. While the house was filled with kin and friends, he lay in his favorite spot under a plum tree. But after all the visitors were gone, he went into the house—which he had never done before without an invitation—and searched every room in the house, upstairs and down. His search was futile, so he went back to his bed under the plum tree and sighed.

As the family grew up and scattered, Billy and Papa spent much time together—two lonely old men, for, as Kirk had said so long before, "Billy is not a dog, he's a *people*." To us, he did indeed seem to be "a people." Billy and Papa were both getting old, and they seemed to realize that they needed each other.

Billy had always had his winter bed in a protected corner of the back porch, but now he was old and stiff with arthritis. Papa put a blanket on the floor in front of the fireplace in his bedroom so Billy could be warm all night, and they could be company for each other.

On a cold day when Papa and Billy were walking down a road rutted in deep snow, a drunken driver came speeding. Papa got out of danger, but Billy's stiff legs failed him and he was hit. He was badly hurt, and Papa carried him to the house. Amy was home from teaching, and she and Papa did all they could for Billy, but in vain. He died in Amy's arms, her tears falling on his wet and muddy fur. They buried him under his plum tree, near Mama's rose garden. ❖

My Dog, My Pal

By George L. "Jerry" Hall

I was born in January 1932. When I was about 8 months old, my mother and father brought home a puppy for me. They named her Pal. Now, Pal didn't do a lot of tricks, but Pal was the perfect name for her. She was always with my brother Jim (who was 13 months younger) and me wherever we went. We walked in the fields and woods during summer and played in snow in the winter. We thought it was great that Pal had puppies every summer. No trick there.

There was one thing, however, for which Pal was well known by most of the people who lived in the small village of LeRoy, N.Y.

My father had a 1932 Pontiac, and he built a platform—complete with windshield—for Pal to ride on (see picture). She loved it! It didn't matter if it was the short, half-mile ride to LeRoy or a long trip, like the two trips we made to spend winter in Florida. She would sit up and look around, and when she got tired, she would lie down and nap. (Keep in mind that in the Good Old Days, there were fewer cars, and we drove much more slowly.)

It was a sad day for me when Pal could no longer jump up onto her riding platform without help. My father finally had to put her down in 1946.

I still miss my Pal. Some of my classmates at class reunions still mention the dog that rode outside the car. ❖

Pal in the spring of 1942.

A Huntin' Dog Named Spot

By Doris Jean Freeman

I was really young at the time, but I can remember seeing my dad's beaming face as he opened the front door. Dad wasn't one to show his emotions, so the fact that he was smiling so broadly made my mom suspicious.

The "surprise" my dad was hiding under his jacket began whining as Dad brought the puppy over to my brother and me.

I glanced at Mom's face. It was clear that she did not share Dad's enthusiasm over this four-legged addition to the family. But somehow, Dad convinced Mom that he could train this scrawny little hound puppy to be the greatest huntin' dog there ever was.

Only later, after a hunting trip in the nearby woods, did Dad discover that Spot—named for the white tip on his tail—was afraid of guns, the sound of gunfire, *anything* to do with hunting. During the years to come, Dad would try to help Spot conquer his fear of guns, but without much success. So much for the "great huntin' dog!" Although Spot enjoyed playing with us kids, he was clearly Dad's dog. Wherever Dad went, Spot was by his side—except, of course, when Dad went hunting.

When it came time for my brother and me to start school that year, we moved from the farm to the so-called rural part of town.

The author's father tried to help Spot overcome his fear of guns.

One lazy summer day, Spot was enjoying the shade of a big oak tree in our back yard. We never knew what triggered it, but the neighbor's dog came running over and lunged at Spot.

Dad ran outside and turned the water hose on both dogs to break up the fight. The neighbor's dog ran off, leaving poor Spot on the ground with a gaping wound on the back of his head.

Dad wrapped Spot in a blanket, gently placed him in the car and sped off to the neighborhood veterinarian. We never had much money, but Dad wanted to do everything he could to save his "best friend." Spot rallied for a while, but he had to be put to sleep when he developed pneumonia.

It was a long, silent ride back home that afternoon. The silence was broken when Dad started talking about how Spot was in "dog heaven" now. Dad did his best to put on a brave face, but his voice began to crack as he spoke about Spot. It was the only time I ever saw my dad cry.

Dad never got another dog. Though Spot never had become a huntin' dog, he *had* become much more. He was a special member of our family, and I'll always remember him as being my dad's best friend. ❖

Four-Legged Delivery Boy

By Edna P. Bates

"To train a dog, you must know more than the dog," my father always affirmed. Mickey was living proof that my father was no slouch mentally! Mickey was a brown-and-white collie, my son's Christmas gift when he was 3, from his grandfather. It was amusing to watch the parade they made. As I was a widow, my son, Joe, followed his grandfather everywhere. He tried to stretch his short legs to step in his grandfather's tracks across the snowy yard. Behind Joe, Mickey bounced from one track to the next. Occasionally he didn't jump high enough and was buried in the snow! It never discouraged him from following his masters, senior and junior.

We lived on a farm on the brow of the Niagara Escarpment. The *Hamilton Spectator* was thrown off a truck at the end of our lane each night. Our dog was trained to bring the rolled-up paper to the door. On a cold afternoon, it was no treat to bundle up, slog through the snow to the road, then find, perhaps, that the truck had been late—and repeat the whole process later on. It was much easier and more pleasant to listen to a scratch on the door, open it, and let the dog bring in the paper. He was happy with his "pay"—a slice of bread or a bone. There was never a suggestion of going on strike for two slices or a bigger bone!

> *"To train a dog, you must know more than the dog," my father always affirmed.*

When he first arrived, however, Mickey couldn't bring the *Spectator* for awhile for several reasons. First, his mouth was too small to go around the roll of paper! Second, his legs were too short to get through the snowbanks alone. However, by spring, his training began.

"Mickey, bring up the paper," my dad said, and my son put it in the puppy's mouth. Mickey promptly dropped the paper. The whole process was repeated, over and over. Soon, Joe and Mickey could go out together when my dad said, "Mickey, go and get the paper." Then the pup learned to go alone, no matter who sent him, and bring the paper to us.

Soon, however, he did more than that. He seemed to know what time the truck came. He would hear it long before we could, and he would mosey out to the road, ready to grab the paper the minute the driver threw it out. Then he would trot up the lane, scratch on the back door, hand it to whoever opened it, and wag expectantly for his reward. However, he never watched for the paper on Sunday!

The *Spectator* drivers used to watch for him. One day a photographer came out from the paper to take a picture of him delivering the paper on the doorstep. They printed the photo in the *Spectator*.

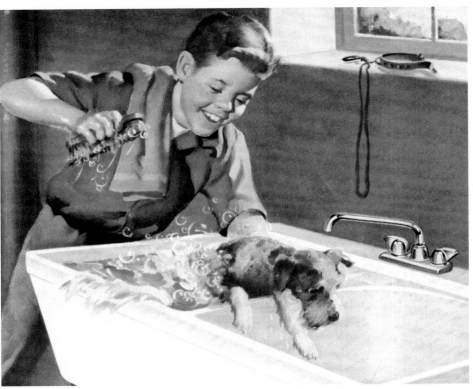

1948 Crane Plumbing and Heating ad, House of White Birches nostalgia archives

Teaching a dog isn't too hard, but getting him to forget it is another matter! One summer when money was scarcer than usual, my dad quit taking the *Spectator*. However, Mickey couldn't seem to get the message. He was used to bringing in a paper about 5 o'clock each day, and he continued to do so.

When we checked it out, we found that he just went to the next-door neighbor's lane and picked up his paper! My dad scolded him, and Joe delivered the paper to Steve, its rightful owner. But the next night, Mickey brought another paper—and we went through the whole thing again.

Scolding and being spanked with the paper finally stopped Mickey from delivering the *Spectator*. However, my dad kept finding them buried in the hay in the barn. Steve wasn't getting his papers at all—even secondhand! At last, in the interest of good neighborly relations, we were forced to renew our subscription so Mickey could deliver his nightly paper legally!

Mickey had more white fur than brown, and his daily activities left him looking rather grubby. His masters put him in a laundry tub full of warm water in the back yard. Surprisingly enough, he submitted quite willingly to his baths. When they poured pails of clear rinse water over him, he sat there with a look of blissful enjoyment on his expressive face.

Wherever Joe went, he was followed by his four-legged shadow. Our fruit farm ran from the Ridge Road right to the top of the Niagara Escarpment. In the spring, we always made several trips to the woods, then down the rocky side of the escarpment to pick wildflowers. Whenever Mickey saw us start back the "green lane" with a basket, he would dash madly ahead of us, knowing his favorite trip was beginning.

While Joe and I picked flowers and filled our basket with rooted plants for our wildflower garden behind the house, Mickey would slither down the steep incline, starting little avalanches of earth and rocks. He would follow the scents of rabbits, squirrels and groundhogs, rushing back every once in awhile to be sure we were still there.

Mickey loved to ride in our truck. He didn't bother about the car, but whenever anyone headed for the truck, he was there ahead of them, waiting to get in. If there was a passenger in the cab, he rode on the floor at his feet, but if the driver was alone, Mickey rode proudly on the seat, looking all around at the scenery with great interest.

When we picked fruit, he would go to the pile of baskets in the orchard and bring one to us whenever he was asked. He loved fruit— cherries, plums and peaches. However, he couldn't manage a whole apple. He liked to eat a piece if you *cut* it off for him. Apparently he preferred the personal touch!

My aunt and uncle lived next-door, nearly a quarter mile away. Our mail had to be picked up at the post office each day. As they had no car, we would get theirs at the same time. We trained Mickey to be a "delivery boy." We tied their mail into a bundle and put it in his mouth. We told him, "Take it to Aunt Hattie."

At first, Joe and Mickey took it together, walking along the end of the grapery, not on the road, to be safe. Soon Mickey could go alone, trotting along to her door. He would scratch on it to announce his arrival. She "paid" him generously with his favorite table scraps. (He never did taste dog food!)

One day, my aunt was away, and no one answered the door. Mickey didn't want to bring her mail back, nor let it blow away. There was a pail of water by the back door, so he dropped it in there!

We wondered if our dog would deliver food or whether he might be tempted to stop and sample it. We put several fresh rolls in a bag, tied a string around it, and said, "Take it to Aunt Hattie." She phoned to say they had arrived safely. The final acid test was a little package of fresh liver, the day my dad butchered a pig. Mickey came through with flying colors—the liver was delivered!

Though Mickey understood English perfectly, he had a little more difficulty speaking it. One spring morning, my dad donned rubber boots and went back to the top of the escarpment to trim peaches.

As the morning wore on and it became warmer, the boots felt hot and uncomfortable. My dad didn't want to waste time walking all the way up to the house, so he wrote a note, tucked it into his mitt with a piece sticking out a hole in the thumb, put it in Mickey's mouth, and told him, "Take it up to Edna."

February 1953. Joe, age 6, with Mickey. Joe wears Grandpa's hat. He and his three cousins, plus Grandma and Grandpa, are ready for Sunday school.

I heard a scratching at the back door and found my dad's "delivery boy." I read his note: "Put my shoes in a basket and send them back with Mickey." I put a shoe in each end of a fruit basket; Mickey took the handle in his mouth and headed back to the peach orchard. Soon my dad was wearing his shoes!

When Joe began school, Mickey would watch for him at the end of the lane each night, then run down the road to meet him. Later, when Joe had to go 5 miles on a school bus, Mickey would hear the bus coming and be waiting at the road when he got off.

With his young master away all day, the dog stayed with my father. Wherever he was working, Mickey was sure to be there too.

When they were both getting old, the farm land was sold. My dad still had his garden and flowers to tend. Mickey would lie beside him, then get up stiffly and move ahead with him every once in a while. When my dad sat on the veranda to cool off, Mickey would sit beside him, close enough to have his head patted. When he became too stiff to climb the three steps, he lay at the bottom of them, waiting for my dad to come down.

Eventually Mickey developed a growth which was obviously giving him pain. He would look at us hopefully, as if to say, "I know *you'll* help me." Finally, a decision had to be made.

One day Mickey went for a ride in his favorite truck with my dad. He couldn't climb any more, so he was lifted in. With his nose on his master's foot, he rode to the animal hospital. He walked in trustingly, knowing that where his master was, he was safe. With my dad's hand on his head, Mickey hardly felt the prick of the needle. He sighed and, his pain gone forever, he collapsed at my dad's feet, where he had spent so many happy hours. ❖

Patience Pays Off

By Audrey Corn

Desperate situations called for desperate measures. If Mama and Papa wouldn't get me a puppy, maybe Santa would. I'd been begging for months for a dog, ever since my big cousin Emmy got hers. Mama said that what with my new baby sister still needing so much attention, she wasn't up to taking on another responsibility. I countered that it was my pet and I'd look after it. Mama knew better! At the age of 5, I wasn't old enough to do for myself, let alone a tiny puppy.

When Mama showed no sign of caving in to my demands, I cast about for another way to get my dog. We lived in Brooklyn, N.Y., back in the 1940s. Come December, Grandma volunteered to mind the new baby while Mama took me, her big girl, to visit Santa.

Right off the bat, I saw my chance. I'd tell Santa I wanted a dog! Naturally, I didn't breathe a word to Mama for fear she'd put the kibosh on my plan.

"I just want one thing," I said. I emphasized the "one."

Saturday morning I was beside myself with excitement. Mama and I took the West End subway to the 34th Street station in Manhattan and rode the elevator up to the fifth floor of Macy's Department Store.

Up close, Santa cut a striking figure with his thick beard and roly-poly build. His eyes were gentle, though, as he lifted me onto his knee. Santa wanted to know if I'd been a good little girl and obeyed my parents. When I solemnly assured him of my sterling character, he asked me to recite my list.

"I just want one thing," I said. I emphasized the "one."

If Santa saw that I wasn't greedy, mightn't he be more inclined to grant my wish?

"And what one gift do you want?" Santa smiled.

"A puppy," I said.

"You mean a toy animal?" Santa asked hopefully.

I shook my head. "I want a real, live dog. Mama and Papa won't give me one, so I need you to deliver it."

Santa considered his answer carefully. Finally, he spoke. "I can't bring puppies or kittens. My sleigh ride takes too long, and the air up near the stars is too cold. A baby animal would catch his death of pneumonia." Despite my disappointment, I understood the logic of Santa's argument. He urged me to think of an alternative wish and I half-heartedly suggested rabbit-fur mittens like the ones my big cousin Emmy wore. I came away with a small candy cane and a sad face.

Facing page: 1955 Friskies Dog Food ad, courtesy Janice Tate

Mama had stood near enough to overhear my exchange with Santa. Nothing was to be gained by discussing my disappointment, so she didn't mention it. Instead, she took me to Nedick's.

Nedick's was a storefront eatery on the corner of 34th Street near Macy's. The restaurant had been built without seats, so we stood like everybody else, and ate in front of the big plate-glass window that looked out onto the sidewalk.

Crowds of Christmas shoppers hurried past, only inches from our noses. Lunch was a treat, but I wanted a puppy.

I finally got my dog the year I turned 9. By that time, my little sister, Jennie, no longer required constant attention, and Mama could help me walk, feed and train my new pet.

I appreciated the puppy all the more because of the long wait. Growing up in the 1940s, my sister and I knew full well the bitter taste of delayed gratification. But oh, how sweet were the fruits of patience! Patience!

How will my grandkids learn the art of patience in today's frenetic world of fast food and faxes, e-mail and instant credit? I suppose my generation grew up with less. But less seemed like more back in the Good Old Days. ❖

The Tonsil Chase

By Vincent Argondezzi

Growing up in our close-knit neighborhood during the Depression, we learned the meaning of sharing. Fortunately, that included sharing Dr. Cordonna, Dr. Fabri and the greatest surgeon in the world—in our eyes— Dr. Ventura. He handled so many surgical emergencies that his reputation reached beyond our section of the east end of Norristown, Pa., which everyone called "Little Italy." We were proud of that warm and cordial neighborhood.

More than once, these good doctors tended our ills for a thank-you. One day, in this spirit, Dr. Ventura came into the neighborhood and announced that he would do free tonsillectomies on all the children needing them.

The thought of surgery panicked me. I was determined not to be available when the doctor made his appearance.

"Watch him closely, Prince," Mom told my beloved dog. "Make sure he doesn't go downstairs during the night to get a snack."

Well, I was determined to be absent when the good doctor came. I got up early and managed to get out before Prince was aware of my intentions. I headed right for the hideout we had up in the field. It was a sort of cave on a high hill, and it was covered with shrubbery. It was impossible to find if you didn't know where it was.

I sat as far back in the hideout as I could and waited. Occasionally I peeked out to check for searchers. Then it happened. I saw them approaching the hideout. I almost stopped breathing. Leading the group was the good doctor. I couldn't believe it! Immaculately attired, with gold pince-nez spectacles, the renowned surgeon was not only ready to operate, but willing to find the patient! I kept as quiet as possible, but I knew it was hopeless because Prince was with them.

"Please, Prince," I whispered to no avail, "don't lead them to the hideout." But Prince stood in front of the brush at the cave and barked. I didn't have any choice but to come out.

"Prince, why did you show our hideout?"

"It's because he loves you and knows what is going to happen is good for you," said the doctor. He was perspiring and seemed a little winded; this might have been the first time he had chased a patient, and there was a hill to climb.

The operation was performed. I was glad to have it over with. I thanked Dr. Ventura and apologized. "I'm sorry I ran and hid," I said. "It wasn't because I thought you were going to hurt me, because you are a great doctor. I was just afraid I would get real sick."

"Well, everything is all right, Vinny," said the good doctor, "but I'll have to confess that I'm not too good at chasing patients."

Prince barked.

"That means he thinks you are the best, Doctor," I said.

"I'm glad of that," smiled Dr. Ventura. "How are *your* tonsils, Prince?"

Prince took off and we all laughed. ❖

House of White Birches nostalgia archives

Little Dog

By Irene Lynn

She hadn't eaten for more than a week, but I was sure she'd snap out of it. She was a tough little dog, and although she must have been at least 15 years old, I just knew she'd pull through. We patted her a lot and tried to coax her to eat. We told her how sorry we were she wasn't feeling well.

Then, one day, we couldn't find her. All day she was gone. The next day, we looked for her again. My husband, Jack, finally found her in a building, way to the back where we never went. She had gone there to die.

Jack buried her under the old apple tree with all our other pets that had died.

I'm sure Jack was remembering all the little things about her, especially the time he was on crutches and had to walk to strengthen his legs. He would slowly walk down the road and back, Little Dog walking beside him. I was amazed by how she would stick right with him, walking at his pace, never running off like she did when she went for a walk with me. With Jack, she walked slowly beside his crutches, never leaving his side.

I came back to the house and dragged her old box off the porch. There was always a mess around her box. I would put a piece of foam in it for her to lie on, and she would dig at it until there were pieces of foam all over the porch.

No more unsightly old box with pieces of foam spilling out, I thought. *That will be nice!*

As I picked up her food bowl, I thought, *Jack won't have to share his Oreo cookies with Little Dog anymore.* She could hear the crackle of a package of Oreo cookies three rooms away. She would coming running and sit up and beg, looking up at Jack with her big brown eyes.

The experts say sweets—especially chocolate—aren't good for dogs, but it never hurt Little Dog. She was healthy all her life, and she had consumed many pounds of chocolate cookies. *Now we won't have her bothering us by sitting up and begging at the table. How nice!*

I took the broom and started sweeping up all the little hairs that constantly littered the porch. I always wondered how one little short-haired dog could shed so much without going bald! *Well, this is the last time I'll have to sweep up those pesky white hairs. That will be nice, too!*

She was a quiet dog, but if a strange cat, dog, groundhog or skunk trespassed at night, she would bark for hours! And if I went out to scold her, she would run after the offending creature, barking worse than ever, and no amount of calling after her would do any good. *No more barking to wake us up in the night. Nice!*

Then there was the UPS truck. She could hear one a mile away. When I saw her crouched low behind the pine tree by our road, I knew a UPS truck was coming. If I scolded and pointed my finger at her, she would go to her box, but if I didn't happen to see her, she would run out at the truck and chase it the length of our yard.

The driver called her "Little Man-eater," and with good reason. He had to run back to his truck many times with her snapping at his heels. *I guess he'll soon find out that she is gone, and that he can safely walk to our door to deliver our packages. He'll like that!*

I thought of the walks I had to take because Little Dog wanted to go hunting. In winter, when I put on my jacket, or in summer, when I put on my old shoes, she would jump up, her little tail wagging, and off she'd go. But not too far. She would stop and look back to check which direction I was going.

When I asked, "Want to go hunting?" I could almost see her smile. I've gone for a lot of walks I didn't want to take because she would start off when I went outside and I didn't have the heart to disappoint her. *Now I won't have to walk over our fields with Little Dog anymore.*

I paused and thought back on all the things I won't have to bother with now that she was gone. You know what? I say this with a lump in my throat: I'm going to miss all those things. ❖

Fluffy

By Frank Maietta

It was August 1929 when our new home was finished and we moved from Bridge Street to Dixie Avenue in the thriving city of Waterbury, Conn. We were not a large family. There were only Ma, Pa and me. I had two pets, a dog named Fluffy, and a cat Ma had named Suzy. I was 8 years old, and that little white poodle was my constant companion.

Fluffy was due to have a litter of puppies, and by some strange coincidence, Suzy was due to have kittens. We were not really settled into our new place when Fluffy had a litter of three pups. About a week later, Suzy had a family of one. Suzy was a calico cat, and the kitten was marked almost identically. I couldn't get over this, and I watched them closely.

One evening about a week after Suzy had her kitten, Ma called her and called her to let her in for the night, but there was no Suzy. Ma and Pa stayed up quite late, calling Suzy, and finally went to bed.

Wonder of wonders, Fluffy had accepted Suzy!

The next morning, as soon as I had breakfast, I began to search for her. I had no luck. In the meantime, the hungry little kitten mewed constantly. Ma found an eye dropper and tried to feed the kitten warm milk. She was not too successful, but she did manage to get some milk into her.

After several days passed and Suzy did not return, Pa told me to give up my daily search of the woods surrounding our place.

The eye-dropper operation still went on with the kitten, with Ma or Pa getting up during the night to feed it. Ma kept worrying that the kitten would starve, and this caused me great concern. I told several neighbors about the situation, but no one could seem to help.

One day I had to go to the store to buy milk, and I told the store lady about the problem we were having with our new kitten. She asked me to wait a few minutes and went to the back room. When she returned, she had a tiny doll's bottle in her hand. "Give this to your mother, and have her try it." I ran all the way home.

When I told Ma about it and she saw the little doll's bottle with its tiny nipple, she exclaimed, "Why didn't we think of something like this?"

We wasted no time thoroughly washing the bottle and its nipple and heating the milk. Holding our breaths, we tried it out on the kitten. At first she pushed the nipple out of her mouth with her tongue, but as soon as she got a good taste of the sweetened milk, she began to hungrily eat. I was thrilled to see the stream of little bubbles that formed as that hungry little creature worked so hard on that nipple.

Of course, Pa or Ma still had to get up during the night to give the kitten its bottle. Pa kept saying that we had to come up with another idea so the kitten would sleep through the night.

We named the little newcomer Suzy, just like her mother. One day, Ma decided to bring the puppies and Suzy out onto the porch for a sunny airing. As I watched Fluffy nurse her puppies, I got an idea. Looking around to be sure the coast was clear, I picked up Suzy and held her mouth against Fluffy. Fluffy did not like the idea, but I held her down and talked to her. She lay back again, and I went to work with Suzy again. When that kitten got a smell of Fluffy's milk,

there was no holding her. When she had her fill she fell asleep.

I kept petting Fluffy, and then I backed off, still watching her. After a few minutes, she fell asleep, too. I remember tiptoeing into the house, holding my finger to my lips, and taking Ma by the hand, silently leading her out to the porch. I pointed to the box where all the pets were asleep. I can still visualize Ma's stunned look of surprise when she got the picture, her lips forming a silent "Oh!"

I sat on that porch all afternoon, watching. My assurance came when Fluffy began to lick her puppies and, after finishing with them, take a careful lick at Suzy. Wonder of wonders, Fluffy had accepted Suzy!

I couldn't wait for Pa to get home from work. When I saw him down the street, I ran to meet him. I didn't quite know how to tell him the news. Pa had certain fixed ideas about what was and wasn't proper. I ended up by telling him I had a surprise for him.

As we approached the porch, all I said was, "Look!"

Pa stared, and then he uttered his classic expression, "Son of a gun!" Fluffy became the center of attention. None of the neighbors believed the story until they came over to have a look. Fluffy actually raised that kitten, caring for it as though it was one of her puppies.

As the pups and Suzy grew older, she became the target of all the pups' rough-and-tumble antics. Sometimes, when the going got a little rough, Fluffy would growl at the pups and break up whatever game they thought they were playing. She was a real little wonder dog during those Good Old Days of my childhood. ❖

Beans and Tamales

By Beth R. Kiteley

Beans and tamales go together. My dog proved this to me. He was really my brother's dog, and why he was named Beans I don't remember. But Beans he was, and since I was the youngest child—and therefore the one home the most—the dog and I were inseparable companions.

There were other playmates, including our neighbor boys, John and George. They were older, so sometimes I was too little and often the wrong sex to be included in their fun.

But on the day of the tamale man, I was involved, and so was Beans.

To 6-year-old eyes, the man was old, but probably he was middle-aged or younger. He had a little pushcart from which he sold ice cream in the summer and tamales in colder weather. His wife made the tamales, he said, and they smelled wonderful.

The pushcart came through our neighborhood occasionally, but I could only imagine the taste of his wares from the sweet or spicy odors. Ice-cream cones cost a nickel and tamales a dime, but nickels and dimes were simply not available at our house. So when John and George said, "Let's get some tamales," I had to admit sadly that I didn't have any money.

"We'll pay," said John generously. So the three of us, with Beans tagging along, ran out to meet the pushcart man. I watched greedily as he lifted out three fat, spicy-smelling corn-husk bundles. He wrapped them carefully in a piece of newspaper, and John, being the oldest, carried the moist package back to my yard.

Before we could open the bundle, the green door up the street banged open, and the boys' mother called, "John! George! Dinnertime! Right now!" The boys jumped guiltily.

"Here, hide them," said George, pulling aside some branches of our spirea bush.

"Can't we have them for dinner?" I asked, wishfully thinking.

"No! Mom'll be mad!" John thrust the bundle into the bush.

"See you after dinner," he called, and the two scampered off.

Just then, I, too, was called to dinner, and with one last whiff of the ambrosia to come, I ran inside.

Well, you guessed it— Beans didn't go in with me. He stayed outside and ate our tamales. He ate all three and licked the cornhusks clean. He even chewed up part of the newspaper. John, George and I poked sadly at the remains. I picked up one of the cornhusks and sniffed it. It still smelled marvelous. But I still didn't know what the pushcart man's tamales tasted like, and Beans wasn't talking.

"Oh, well," said George, "I'm not hungry anyway. C'mon, let's go play ball!"

"Can I come?" I pleaded.

"No!" was their retort. "You're too little. And your dog's a pig!"

The two boys ran off, calling back, "Pig, pig, pig!" I sat down on the steps beside Beans. He put his head in my lap and belched. ❖

Peg, Our English Setter

By Thomas E. Wirt

I would like to share a story about our English setter, Peg. My dad was an avid quail hunter in the 1920s, '30s and '40s, and he always had a bird dog to hunt with. Peg was one of the very best, and we thought she was as much a part of our family as any brother or sister.

She never failed to meet us as we walked up to the house, always showing a big grin as if she were about to bite.

Our house was one of a dozen on a street in Columbia, Mo. It had been built by my grandfather in 1938—one story, two bedrooms, with a full basement. The whole thing cost $3,800, including the lot.

Dad worked for a trucking company, and we had one of the very few vehicles on the block, a 1939 pickup truck.

Grandpa and Grandma lived about three blocks away, and, since we didn't have a washing machine, my dad would load a basket of dirty clothes in his truck and haul them to their house once a week, leaving them on their front porch early in the morning.

Peg would take a shortcut through the neighborhood to Grandpa's and Grandma's

This photograph of the author's English setter, Peg, was taken in 1942.

and sit on their porch with that basket of clothes until they were picked up and taken inside. Then she would return home. This was a weekly ritual, regardless of the weather, summer or winter.

A good bird dog was hard to find back then, and one fall we nearly lost her.

Quail season opened on Nov. 10, and one morning about two weeks earlier, Peg had gone missing from our back porch.

We searched day and night for a week, but there was no sign of her.

Then, two weeks later, I was playing with several friends in a yard across the street when I heard something under some bushes next to the house.

There was Peg, with a long rope still tied around her neck. Her feet and sides by her legs were covered with blood, and she couldn't walk.

My friends and I carried her across the street to our house, and our family nursed her back to health in the basement. We often wondered how far she had traveled to return home. From then on, she was kept in the house for several weeks before bird season—except for laundry day, of course. ❖

Handy, My Helper and My Friend

By Opal Blaylock

The pet that was more than a playmate was a small, tan, saddleback beagle. He was a gentle, loving, smart and somewhat wimpy fellow I named Handyman. He lived up to his nickname Handy for 17 crucial years of my adult life. He was my helper and my friend. My husband suffered a near-fatal heart attack that left him very weak. The only exercise he could do was walk. He started out walking half a block and back. Then he began adding a few more steps until he was walking all around our neighborhood.

One of our neighbor's dogs had a litter of beagle puppies. Bryant had hunting beagles, and he was interested in the new puppies.

One day he brought a little ball of fur in and handed it to me. "Okay, honey," he said. "Now you have your own beagle."

I wasn't sure I wanted something else to take care of at this point in my life. I had gone back to work after spending weeks at Bryant's bedside and more weeks giving him in-home care. I really thought I had put in enough man-hours in the "care for" department. But as I held that little fur ball and felt him relax and fall asleep in my lap, and I knew he was there to stay. And stay he did for the next 17 years.

Handy stayed very close to us for a couple of weeks. When we felt comfortable leaving him outside, he quickly became the older hunting dogs' little brother. Handy learned quickly how much "puppy play"

> *On more than one occasion, Bryant didn't feel like he could make it back to our house. He would remove the leash and tell Handy, "Go get Mama."*

Mac and Gritty would tolerate. And it only took one little rake of the cat's paw across his nose to send him yelping to me. He never chased or got very close to any cat again for the rest of his days.

When Handy was about 3 months old, he tried to climb over the back fence. When he started to climb, I went around the block and met him at the scene of his crime with a cardboard tube from the center of a roll of paper towels. I never touched him with it; I just whacked my hand with it. Then I set him a couple of feet off the ground onto the fence, and he climbed back into his own space. He never climbed anything again.

By now, Bryant was able to walk a mile or so most days, and he started taking Handy with him. Our close-knit neighborhood watched as "the sick man" recovered, and took note of his new walking buddy.

On more than one occasion, however, Bryant didn't feel like he could make it back to our house. He would remove the leash and tell Handy, "Go get Mama." Handy would run to our front door and bark.

I'd grab the car keys and Handy would beat me to the car, sit on the front seat and look out until I got to wherever Bryant had sat down to wait for us. When Bryant got into the car, Handy would jump to the back, lie down and sigh. He knew his work was done.

As the years passed, Bryant got better, but Handy had his own troubles. One day, as he ran to catch up with Bryant to take a walk, he fell, yelping in pain. We tried to pick him up, but he was just in too much pain. I pulled the truck around, and we picked him up on a quilt and rushed him to the vet. The agony was just about too much for him. Dr. Bondurant came to the truck and gave him a shot and helped us get him into the office.

He even pawed a pillow over to lay his head on! What a pitiful sight!

After getting Handy comfortable, he X-rayed and found two herniated discs in his neck. The doctor soon performed the needed surgery and, of course, kept Handy a couple of days.

But when I went to pick him up to bring him home, he wasn't in his assigned bed. I had a meltdown! I took off to the outer office, crying and sniffling, and when the receptionist saw me, she knew what had happened. They had taken Handy out of his bed to let him walk around, and when he was done, he had simply crawled under her desk and made himself at home at her feet. They put a little rug down for him, and there he lay, resting as if he owned the place.

After we took Handy home, the receptionist often called us to check on him. He had stolen her heart.

One of my favorite stories about him always brings smiles when we tell it. I had taken Handy in for his check-up. His only trouble was that when he walked across the carpet, he yelped. I had checked his feet and found nothing. Dr. Bondurant took a closer look and found that one of his dewclaws was torn just enough to catch on a fiber when he walked across the floor. He put some disinfectant on Handy's foot and quickly snipped off the torn claw. Even though I was holding him, he let out a blood-curdling howl like you wouldn't believe. We petted and soothed him, and Dr. B put some antibiotic ointment and a huge Ace bandage on his foot.

When we got home, Mr. Handy would have no part of the floor. He wanted up on the couch. This was a no-no, but I reneged and put a towel on the couch and put him where he wanted to be. He even pawed a pillow over to lay his head on! What a pitiful sight!

When Bryant came in and saw him lying there, he knelt down in front of him and asked him what had happened. I promise you, Handy shook that big old bandage in Bryant's face and let out the exact same whoop he had produced in the vet's office. I wish I had had the camera ready to catch the expression on Bryant's face.

Handy continued to experience health difficulties. Arthritis plagued him, and I had to give him pills for that. He knew what time his pill was due, and he came to the cabinet every day at the same time to get it. No one believed me when I told them that. When the time came to change the clocks for Daylight Savings Time, Handy didn't know that had taken place and just kept coming at the time he always came.

Even with old age, hearing loss, pain in his joints and heart failure, he remained a sweet, loving, devoted, gentle little friend until that day when a stroke took him where all good doggies go. I treasure my memories of him, with thanks to God for knowing what I needed and when I needed it, and for filling that need with one of His special creations. ❖

A Special Dog

By Anne J. Basile

For thousands of years, dogs and their owners have shared a strong bond. I can verify that; I've felt that bond with my dogs since I was a small child. When I was 4, my mother was diagnosed with tuberculosis and was placed in a sanatorium. Complete bed rest, isolated from family and friends, was the only treatment.

Not understanding her sudden disappearance, I was inconsolable. It was then that Skippy, a black-and-white fox terrier, entered my life and became my confidant and constant companion. He seemed to sense when I was unhappy, and he would jump into my lap and gaze at me with questioning eyes. It was easier to tell my troubles to him than to my father or older sister.

When I cried, he licked the tears from my face. During bouts of measles, mumps and chicken pox, he was better medicine than doctors could prescribe. Hugging him close made life bearable.

My mother was allowed to come home toward the end of her life, but she was still bedfast and isolated. When school was out, I was expected to be quiet for her sake, but that was impossible for a rambunctious 10-year-old. Fortunately, my grandfather came to the rescue and invited me to spend the summer on his farm—and of course, Skippy went with me.

Life was entirely different at his house. The barnyard was surrounded by cotton fields and woods. We could run free to search for guinea hens' speckled eggs, chase rabbits, groundhogs and squirrels, and dig for worms to fish in the creek. More than once, Skippy's excited bark

Skippy and the author in 1927.

saved me from a dangerous water moccasin.

We'd get up at dawn to ride in the buggy with Grandpa while he delivered milk or drove into town. At night, when I was homesick, I could reach for Skippy sleeping beside me. Together we enjoyed a carefree and renewing summer, one of the happiest of my childhood.

Back home again, everything changed. Several caretakers came and went, unable to cope with a tubercular invalid and four energetic children. Skippy remained the only constant during those chaotic days, a reliable source of comfort.

The strong bond I forged with Skippy was repeated with all seven dogs that followed him. My dogs enriched my life for 70 years. I wouldn't have been the same without them. ❖

Old Friends

By Mamie LeVan

The man was aged and gnarled and bent,
The dog his constant companion and friend.
Oh, what a threesome through snow and rain—
The man, the dog and the twisted old cane.
Times have changed, the dog is gone,
And now the old man walks alone.
No more wagging tail by his side.
His constant companion grew feeble and died.
The man grew older as years went on;
He withered and weakened and now *he's* gone.
Alas, this chapter has come to an end.
Farewell to the man and his trusty old friend!

Spotty Dog

By Glen Herndon

How well I remember our Navy chowline on Guam, 1950, for we always had visitors while standing in line: a big old yellow dog named Laddy, who was a big flirt, courting us for handouts; and then, a new arrival someone started calling "Spotty Dog." He answered to it, especially if he came up to you on the way out and you'd brought him a treat, like a piece of your roast beef dinner!

So Spotty Dog it was. No one knew where he came from, and he belonged to nobody. He simply declared himself our mascot, and that was that! He spent his whole day wandering around the barracks and sleeping off all those snacks. He grew plump and lazy, but you couldn't call him sleek because his short white coat was dirty.

We guessed he had been some Navy family's pet, and they had left him behind when they were shipped back stateside. They could have sent him home, but there was some expense and paperwork involved; perhaps, like so many, they just didn't bother.

Oh, there were lots of dogs on Guam in those Good Old Days. All the better for us homesick sailors who had left pets behind. We heard there was even a veterinary hospital being set up by the Navy to provide some care for them.

One day, Spotty Dog visited our barracks. We were the crew of printers, journalists and so on that put out the Navy newspaper, the *Guam News*, way out there in the Pacific.

Spotty Dog ignored the rest of us and went right over to Jim Campbell, who sat on his bunk, writing a letter. Jim was a quiet redhead with freckles and a Southern drawl. Putting his pen and paper aside, he reached out for Spotty Dog's ears and massaged them gently. "Dogs allus like this," Jim said. "Hi, Spotty Dawg! Y'all decide to come visit me fin'ly?"

It was plain to see that those two hit it off right away, and that was good because Jim was undoubtedly one of the loneliest guys on the base. He was quiet and unassuming, and though friendly enough, he didn't seem to have any pals.

This photo of Spotty Dog was taken by Glen Herndon while serving in Guam in 1950. Spotty Dog was the company mascot. Spotty liked everyone, but he loved Jim Campbell. Jim brought him back stateside to live "on the backside of nowhere" in Louisiana.

Was Spotty Dog attracted to him because he was like his former master? It didn't matter. Jim said, "Spotty Dog, you are a sight, and you need a bath, an' we gonna git one right now—me and you! We'll be down to the showers, fellas."

A couple of minutes later, that is just where they headed, Jim wearing one towel

Jim Campbell and Spotty Dog entertain a canine friend in the barracks on Guam in 1950. Photo by Glen Herndon.

and carrying an extra to dry Spotty Dog, along with a big can of bath talc.

This was the first time any of us could remember a dog getting a shower, but leave it to comical little Jim, whose down-home phrases like "Your foot in a fat gourd!" kept us all smiling. Jim was shy and didn't think he fit in, but the fact was we laughed *with* him and not *at* him.

He returned with a much nicer dog following him, and you could see Spotty Dog was the happiest he'd been in a long time. He felt good! After that, just about every day, he wanted his shower and bath talc, too, just like Jim had.

We rode down the hill to our newspaper plant in a ton-and-a-half stake truck equipped with benches. The truck ran a regular shuttle service between us and the quarters on the hill, and one man was assigned as driver. On the next trip down to the plant, Jim went along and

brought Spotty Dog, who promptly became mascot of our production crew.

There was no disliking Spotty Dog. Everyone spoiled him—petting and giving him treats out of our big refrigerated food chests.

Our publisher and officer-in-charge was Navy Lt. David Martin, sent out from the Pentagon in Washington, D.C., where he had been in Navy Personnel. He took an interest in every one of us who worked for him, and he noted how bonding with Spotty Dog had brought Jim out of his shell so that he was more sociable.

Lt. Bob Strahl set up one of his famous beach parties at Tumon Bay, where there was great swimming in the shallow reef lagoon. None of us was surprised when Spotty Dog was out there, dog-paddling with Jim and having a wonderful time.

Jim did one thing that irritated Spotty Dog. When he played one of his country records such as *Six More Miles to the Graveyard, Six More Miles Left to Ride,* Spotty Dog listened—until someone started playing the Jew's harp or harmonica or began yodeling. Then he'd howl as if singing along. In truth, it probably hurt his ears.

Jim's friendship with the dog seemed to make him someone special to everyone, giving him a kind of special status. Jim was a graduate of Navy Printer's School, but he was lowest man on the print-shop totem pole. He got all the dirty clean-up jobs, but he never let it bother him. He just sang his favorite country songs to Spotty Dog and always had a ready smile. Now he seemed at ease and felt like he really belonged.

But we all knew changes were afoot. The Navy decided to sell the *Guam News* to George Armitage of Honolulu, a civilian publisher. By midsummer, the sale was done, and the Navy staff were reassigned. Jim and the other printers were sent down to the Navy area print shop. Others, including me, were reassigned to headquarters command and stayed where we were.

Once in a while, we wondered about Jim and Spotty Dog. We always got a report that they were doing fine and as happy as ever.

I went off early in 1951 on a series of special assignments. When I got back, I heard that Jim's enlistment was up, and he would be heading stateside for discharge. He had made arrangements to send Spotty Dog to the States, too. Awhile later, we heard that he had written a letter from his bayou country town that he always said was "on the backside of nowhere." He wrote that he and Spotty Dog were still enjoying each other. Spotty Dog liked the warm Louisiana summer weather; he seemed to think he was still on tropical Guam. The two of them, Jim and Spotty Dog, just went around boondockin' and having a good time.

Jim reported that Spotty Dog couldn't be trained as a hunter; he was too old and not mean enough. Why, he even wanted to be friends with a 'gator! As usual, Jim's words made us smile. ❖

The Rest of the Story

By Ken Tate, Editor

Radio journalist and commentator Paul Harvey has a daily feature that Janice and I love. It's called "The Rest of the Story," and he always ends his program with: "And now you know *the rest* of the story." I'd like to share the rest of Spotty Dog's story with you.

"Spotty Dog" originally appeared in the September 2004 issue of *Good Old Days*. That issue made its rounds and ended up in the hands of Guy Shine, a retired lieutenant colonel who flew B-29 bombers out of Guam during World War II. When Lt. Col. Shine read the story of Spotty Dog, he said immediately, "I know that dog!"

Spotty Dog matched the description and age of a puppy brought to Guam in 1945 by the crew of a B-29 in Lt. Col. Shine's 330th Bomber Group. Lt. Col. Shine sent me the photo below, taken on April 9, 1945, in Peyote, Texas, before the bomber was deployed. It shows the puppy mascot that the crew named Putt-Putt. Scratching the puppy's ear is the crew's commander, Lt. Donald Schiltz.

Tragically, the Schiltz B-29 was shot down over Kobe, Japan, on June 5, 1945, and the entire crew died. Lt. Col. Shine says he remembered that Putt-Putt became a vagabond after the loss of Lt. Schiltz and his crew.

The puppy was befriended by different people, but apparently was still a vagabond when Jim Campbell adopted him five years later.

So the little mascot Putt-Putt became Spotty Dog, the best friend of Jim Campbell in the bayous of Louisiana. I hope he lived out a peaceful, long life back in the Good Old Days. "And now you know the rest of the story." ❖

Front row: Leonard Holm, Lt. Donald Schiltz, Lt. Anthony Picciano, Lt. Robert Scott, Pvt. Putt-Putt (front and center). Back row: Sgt. George Reed, Cpl. David Grunigen, Sgt. Francis Boulay, James Dill (replaced by PFC Byron Chatum in Guam), Sgt. Woodrow Collins, Cpl. James Davidson.

To the Rescue

Chapter Two

Grandma Stamps' brother, Sherman Blevins, was more than a great-uncle to me. He was a "Great Uncle" as well—a man I idolized. Being my grandmother's brother meant he was considerably older than my other uncles. By the time I was old enough to spend time with him, he was retired, so he could dote a bit on me.

Uncle Sherman didn't live very far from us—a little over a mile down the road—but that didn't mean I got to spend as much time with him as I wished I could.

He had a small farm, with a gigantic pond out back of his home. (At least it seemed gigantic to me!) When I did get to visit, I usually talked Uncle Sherman into taking me to fish for the perch and small bass that populated his pond.

We made quite a parade, I'm sure. Uncle Sherman led the way, tall and lanky; he carried whatever fishing gear he thought we might need. I followed, usually clad in overalls. My pockets were usually full of worms and my head full of questions for my sage uncle.

"Uncle Sherman, will we be able to catch any cats plantin' cattails in your pond?"

"Uncle Sherman, when do frogs quit being fish and grow legs?

"Uncle Sherman, …?"

He usually quieted me by pointing out that noise would scare the fish away.

The end of the parade was the faithful farm dog. I don't remember his name; I just remember thinking that he must have been trained to follow and keep me on the straight and narrow path leading from Uncle Sherman's house to the pond.

One such outing was an idyllic summer day. The fish were biting and the mosquitoes were not. Everything was perfect until I snagged a bigger-than-average perch and, in my excitement, lost my balance and tumbled headlong into the deep water of the pond.

> *I never knew if Uncle Sherman ordered his dog to the rescue, or if he just did it instinctively.*

Without a moment's hesitation, Uncle Sherman's dog was in the water with me, pulling me up by the overalls and then paddling toward the bank. I never knew if Uncle Sherman ordered his dog to the rescue, or if he just did it instinctively when he heard my cry.

Uncle Sherman met us at the bank and finished the rescue mission. I had lost a shoe and cried that Daddy would have my hide if I came home without it. So, Uncle Sherman's dog was sent back into the warm water of the pond. My shoe was a little the worse for wear when he pulled it out, but at least I still had it.

That was twice in the same day that pooch rescued me.

The stories that follow are filled with heroism and poignancy. Whether they tell of pets helping people, people helping pets or pets helping each other, all will remind you of the scripture: "Greater love hath no man [or animal] than this, that a man lay down his life for his friends." (John 15:13)

And that's what happened when friends came to the rescue in the Good Old Days.

—Ken Tate

And the Wind Began to Blow

By Kathy Woodard

The day had been stormy, rain mixed with sleet and snow. It was January 1937 in west Tennessee, along the lowlands of the Mississippi River. "Daddy, what is the glitter and shine over in the woods?" I asked.

"It's called backwater, sister. The river has flooded out of its banks, and the water is seeking its level in the low places."

I gazed at the strange sight. The sun had shone through a rift in the dark clouds and set off a myriad of sparkles and flashings in the nearby woods. I finished gathering the box of wood chips and went into the kitchen with the last armload of wood for the cookstove.

I told my sister and baby brother about the water and asked Mother if it would come any closer to us. She didn't think so, as our house sat on a high knoll. When chores were finished, Mother put supper on the table while Daddy and I washed up.

As I huddled under the quilt, my little dog crept into my bed and snuggled.

Just before sunset, dark clouds once again covered the sky and a fierce wind began to blow. We ate supper by the light of a kerosene lamp, listening to the wind.

After the dishes were washed and put away, we went into the living room, where Daddy had a cheerful fire going. My sister and I had school work to do; Mother was rocking Baby and singing softly to him.

Daddy laid aside the half-finished oar he was working on and walked to the front door. He heard a rushing noise that didn't sound like the wind. He slammed the door and hurried back into the room.

"Pearl, get warm coats on the children and pack a few things; the water is in the yard!" Daddy grabbed his raincoat off the hook and rushed out into the night. He set out for his boat tied on a small pond nearly half a mile away where he fished and hunted. It was a small rowboat he had made himself only a short time ago, and he had not finished the oars yet. We watched anxiously from the window as he waded out into the dark, swirling water.

The storm grew into a howling monster, hurling rain, sleet and snow against our house. Daddy returned, soaked and half-frozen. He couldn't make it to the boat. The floodwater was rising too fast and was full of uprooted trees and other debris. He changed into dry clothes and sat by the fire. Mother made hot coffee and they talked in low voices.

Bedtime came. Mother made us pallets of featherbeds on the floor near the big heater. We were too fearful to go to our beds while the storm raged so fiercely! As I huddled under the quilt, listening to the lash of the wind and rain, my little dog crept into my bed and snuggled under the quilt with me. I fell asleep, hugging his little warm body for comfort. I doubt my parents slept at all that night.

By the grayness of dawn, Mother had breakfast on the table. Daddy looked worried as he helped put away the bedding. He told of a levee that had broken late yesterday afternoon. This had let a lot of extra water in our area. We dressed in our warmest clothes, knowing help would be arriving soon after sunup.

The sun rose weakly. The storm of last night was gone, but the sky was still cloudy. After breakfast, we looked out the window. There was no earth anywhere—just water as far as we could see! Water lapped at our doorsteps.

I was 8 years old and filled with dread. I watched my parents' faces, my mind racing with unasked questions. Would our house float away? Would it sink and take us with it? Would it topple over into the water and leave us sitting on the bare floor like a large raft?

Daddy seemed brave, but he never smiled. Mother's hands were fluttery. My little sister had had polio two years earlier, and Mother was dividing time between my sister's needs and baby brother, so I kept my questions to myself.

About midmorning, we heard the chug of a sputtering motor. Daddy stood on the porch in the cold to call to the boatman. He manned one of many boats sent to find and rescue stranded flood victims. The motor had given him trouble and he was returning to land. Mother dressed us in woolen, two-piece snowsuits and packed a change of clothing in an old, scruffed bag.

Before I was helped into the boat, I tucked my little dog in the bib of my snowpants and buttoned my coat over him. I sat on a crossboard in the middle of the boat. Daddy wrapped a quilt around Mother and my sister, sitting in the front of the boat with baby brother on Mother's lap. He placed the bag of clothing and the shotgun near my feet.

Thus we set out on a 17-mile journey over turbulent water through stormy weather. We couldn't make much distance before night. The water was filled with uprooted trees and all kinds of floating objects that caused the motor to clog. Often the men had to row and push the boat away from things that floated too near.

By midafternoon, the sky had turned to a lead gray. It started to snow. We had to reach some kind of shelter and soon. We would never survive if we were caught out on open water in such a crippled boat after dark. The men were extremely tired from the mental as well as the physical labor.

Daddy remembered an old, abandoned sawmill not too far from away. They pointed the boat in that direction and rowed with a watchful eye, uncertain if it still stood. The mill had been built on tall, thick pilings

As the boat moved around a clump of thick-branched treetops, we could see the old roof, like an island in a vast ocean! Just before dark, the boat floated under the big roof to a narrow walkway that had been built near the eaves. Daddy climbed up onto the wide boards and helped each of us out of the boat. He held onto us until we walked about a bit and were steadier on our feet. We had only one quilt and the warmth of the adults to keep us warm. There was no food, and my baby brother cried himself to sleep.

My little dog ran about, barking at the little feathered creatures that shared our haven for the night, perched beneath the roof. Daddy sang us to sleep with cowboy ballads and love songs like *Barbara Allen* and a fractious boy named *Freckles* who got blamed for everything. Somehow, we fell asleep.

About an hour after daylight, there was still no sun, but in the distance toward the east, where land should be, there was a steady drone of motors. Daddy and the boatman climbed up onto the tin roof of the old mill. Nobody could see us underneath, on the walkway. The water was too high and the shadows too thick.

When a boat appeared on the horizon, the men shouted and waved a shirt. When the large boat coasted under the roof, Mother cried wracking sobs of relief, hugging her children to her. Once again, we started to safety with the small boat and its bad motor in tow. The water was calmer now, and the wind had died. Spread out over the water, we saw several boats filled with flood victims like us, headed for safety. We learned that one family had clung in a treetop all night, waiting and praying for help to come.

A loud cheer went up when land was sighted. But as the boats drifted onto shore, it started snowing again. Thick, swirling flakes made vision difficult. There was a mad scramble as the boats were unloaded. Legs were cramped and stiff. There were belongings to be gathered and children to be kept track of—and shelter was still more than a half mile away. Everyone set out at a fast trot, hurrying toward food and a warm fire!

My grandpa's house and that of a favorite uncle were among the first homes we reached. Grandpa and Uncle Jim waited at the water's edge with several neighbors to welcome the homeless to food and shelter.

When our boat slid up onto the sand and mud, I was jerked off the board I was sitting on. I landed on my backside in the bottom of the boat. About a gallon of water sloshed into the hull between the ribs of the boat.

My wool snowsuit soaked up the freezing water like a sponge. When I stood up, the cloth froze to my body. Worse, I was separated from my parents in the throng of hurrying people.

Everyone was gone and I was alone in the wet, blinding snow. Tears filled my eyes as I looked down at my little dog shivering at my feet. I picked him up and stuffed him into the bib of my snowpants, then buttoned my jacket up snug under my chin.

I picked up Daddy's shotgun that was leaning against the boat and walked in the direction of the voices of the people who were hurrying away. The sound grew fainter as the distance between us grew. I tried to call after them, but no sound came from my fear-clogged throat! The snow was falling faster and too thickly for me to see very far ahead. I felt lost and abandoned. The gun grew heavy, and my steps were

slowed. I was so tired. I wanted to lie down and sleep, *just for a few minutes*.

I staggered near the side of the road, slid, then tumbled into a deep ditch. The water in the ditch was frozen and snow had drifted in to fill it completely. As I slid under the snow, I went into a deep sleep, hugging my little dog tightly.

When the others reached shelter, they gathered into family groups. Uncle Jim stood on his porch and called out: "Have any of you seen Kat? Did she go on to Papa's house?"

No one remembered seeing me since the boats were unloaded! Daddy and Mother assumed I was with Uncle Jim. His home was my favorite place other than my own.

A short distance up the road toward the houses, Uncle Jim heard the faint whine of a dog.

Uncle Jim grabbed a sheep-lined coat and set off for the landed boats. He hurried through the snow, searching each step of the road from side to side. By the time he neared the boats, he had found nothing. He began to call my name, listening after each call.

A short distance up the road toward the houses, he heard the faint whine of a dog. He dug us out of the hole and carried us in his arms all the way home. When I awoke, I was in Aunt Ester Lee's kitchen, being rubbed with snow to thaw my frozen body. They had fed my dog and he was sleeping, all snug in a box, behind the stove. The doctor arrived, and together they kept my hands, feet, ears and face from frostbite.

It was spring before I could run and play again with the little friend who had saved my life. Only the warmth of his tiny body had kept my heart warm and had prevented me from freezing to death!

We grew up. The little dog lived to a ripe old age. When he died, I knew I had lost my very best friend.

The emotional scars are deep from that ordeal. It happened more than 50 years ago, and still the bad dreams sometimes haunt me. When I drive on a bridge over a river, the choking fear rushes like wind over my skin! I realized how deep my fear of water was when I drove across the great Mackinac Bridge linking Michigan's Upper and Lower Peninsulas. Never again! Please, God, never again! ❖

Bingo Was His Name

By Carol S. Waldon

I grew up in a small town called Ardmore, Md. It had a Protestant church, a Catholic church, one small grocery store and a school. My family and I lived on a small farm. My father had outside work as the farm alone couldn't support our family. My family consisted of Daddy, Momma, my brother Tommy and me. We had several animals on the farm, but mainly one indoor cat and three dogs, Red, Jinx and Jigs. This particular story pertains to the cat, Bingo.

He was a big orange tom cat and not particularly affectionate. He called the shots when it came to petting him. He did love my mother, and if she handed him any of the food she was eating, he would eat it.

It was Easter Sunday. My folks were going out for the evening with another couple, and their son Dinks was going to spend the evening with Tommy and me. Tommy was 15 or 16 years old at the time, as was Dinks. We were sprawled across my parents' bed, listening to murder mysteries on the radio.

Before my parents left the house, they had warned my brother about not lighting the kitchen light on the way to the bathroom. Some renovations were being done on the house, and the electrical wiring wasn't hooked up properly yet. But sometime during the evening, one of us kids must have forgotten and turned the light on. As the night went on, we ended up falling asleep on the bed while the radio was still playing.

Unbeknownst to us, an electrical fire had started in the wiring, and the walls were on fire. Bingo jumped on our friend's chest and

House of White Birches nostalgia archives

started licking his face. Dinks wasn't particularly fond of cats, and he woke up right away and smelled the smoke. He woke Tommy, and we all ran out into the driveway to one of the cars that was parked there. Fortunately, the car was quite a distance from the house.

As we watched flames coming out of the roof, I cried for Tommy to go get my Easter basket. He did go into the house and retrieve a blanket for me and a metal box that contained important papers. As he was running out of the house, the roof collapsed, but he managed to get out in time.

One of the neighbors on the next farm had seen the flames and had called the fire department. Since it was volunteer, it took a long time to get to the house. The building was pretty much gone by the time they arrived. By then, the fire was too close to the well just behind the house, where they needed to get the water.

By the time all this was happening, many people saw the smoke for miles around and started driving in the direction of our farm. Our parents were in that crowd, and for a while, they didn't know it was their house that was burning. When they finally got to our lane, they had to restrain my mother to keep her from jumping out of the moving car. As soon as she found out that Tommy, Dinks and I were safe, she was OK.

We didn't see Bingo for several days and thought he had been burned in the fire. Days later, however, he returned to the farm and was quite the hero. He lived with us for many more years in the garage that was made over into a house for us.

That's the story of my favorite pet! ❖

Tobias Tugmutton

By Joan E. Dickson

Our family never had dogs while I was growing up, but we had a few cats. One cat that stands out in my memory was Tobias Tugmutton. You probably think that is rather a strange name for a cat, so I will tell you how he received it.

In the 1940s, I read a book about a little girl who named her cat Tobias Tugmutton. She nicknamed him Toby, but sometimes Toby did naughty things, and when he was naughty, she would call him Tobias. I liked that story very much, so when a male tabby cat came into my life, I decided to call him that.

Toby was a fun cat and a very amiable playmate. He would allow me to dress him in doll clothes and push him around the yard in a doll buggy. We had tea parties with my dolls. I hardly ever had to call him Tobias, he was such a good cat.

We were living in a mining town in Idaho at that time, and we were snowed in for much of the winter. When spring arrived and the snow melted, the creek that ran near our house was full of rapidly flowing water.

There was a bridge that crossed the creek not too far from where we lived, and one day, I heard a commotion on the bridge. When I looked over, there was Toby and another male cat having a cat fight.

I was astonished to see my gentle cat in a fight! Certainly he wasn't any match for the other ferocious male. My worst fears came true when Toby was thrown off the bridge and into the rushing water. I ran to the creek bank, but I was unable to rescue him.

About that time, I noticed a dog standing on the edge of the bank. He saw Toby, quickly jumped in, dog-paddled over and pulled him to safety. His reward for saving Toby was a scratch on the nose.

I was very glad to have my cat back, but I formed the opinion that cats can be ungrateful creatures. For the rest of that day, he was known as Tobias Tugmutton! ❖

Right: The author and the infamous Tobias Tugmutton.

The Bold Adventurer

By A.S. Gleason

A country boy who would have been terrified by town traffic, not to mention city traffic, was a bold adventurer in his own home territory. This was especially true when he had a city cousin visiting. Commonplace, everyday experiences could, with a bit of skillful suggestion, take on the aura of true adventure.

A girl called Margie was the first to come under my bold spell. She was a small, blond, rather timid child, allowed very little freedom by her semi-invalid mother. She was sent to our place for a summer because her mother, for whom my father had very little use, was sick. My mother had a great affection for the little girl and vowed to "put roses in her cheeks."

At first, Margie spent most of her time sitting on the veranda, perpetually afraid of getting in someone's way. I had been instructed to try to get her to play. I wasn't to introduce any rough games, however. She smiled shyly at each suggestion and stayed in the chair.

"Margie, why don't you run on and play?" suggested my mother.

Margie then transferred herself from the back stoop to the bench beside the driving shed. I brought out in succession the riches of my play equipment. There was an old steering wheel from a car, bent but quite usable for playing car; a bent steel buggy hoop; three or four barrel staves; a boat Grandfather had carved from a piece of cedar; a sponge-rubber ball; a jackknife with a broken blade; a cigar box full of colored stones; two broom handles and a wad of frayed Sunday comics. Nothing, however, seemed to stir the girl.

When I confessed my failure to Grandfather, he nodded and said he would get her playing. He vanished at noon and reappeared at about 1:30, carrying a puppy in his arms. Without saying a word, he dumped the pup into the little girl's arms. It was absolutely magical to see the change in the child. She laughed and cried alternately for about a half hour.

My mother smiled and beckoned me into the house. "Margie will be a fine playmate now. You see, that child needs to either love or be loved. Poor thing hasn't had much of either."

That changed the course of the summer. Margie was game to go anywhere, just as long as she could carry Spots with her. He was a small, runty puppy of indeterminate origin, but the grand champion of all the canine world couldn't have displaced him in the affections of Margie.

Even our old collie seemed to sense the situation. He didn't put up any fuss about the pup. The four of us wandered through the fields

and the swale and the bush. We played pirates on the raft on the old pond in the pasture, and we poked for frogs and toads in the cold, musty darkness of the creek culvert.

I led an adventurous expedition to the gravel pit, and we buried treasure in the old cave on the side of the brickyard hill. I cut willow wands and bent pins for fishing hooks, and even Margie caught a diminutive chub, which Mother, with all solemnity, fried for her breakfast. We climbed the beams in the barn and became infested with barn lice.

At that tender age, I could imagine myself as a combination of every hero I had ever heard of. The pools, the valley and the creek became the settings for untold adventures. Something else was happening, too. Margie, who gave me tribute as the acknowledged leader, was changing a great deal.

I noticed that she no longer clung to the pup, who by this time had developed into a capering, frolicking creature. Margie climbed trees, fell into the creek and picked suckers from her arms and legs without squealing. She scrambled over rocks, stuffed herself with berries and choke-cherries, and followed me into the darkest spot of the old cave.

Her face was browning and freckled. Her hands had calluses, and her tender feet could even negotiate the gravel-pit stones. She ate with gusto and slept the night through with no trace of the shadows that had haunted her when she first came to our place.

The day she left for the city, I fled to the back of the barn. It would never have done for me to be seen crying. It was out of character for a bold adventurer to cry over a girl. ❖

Saved by a Pig

By Doyle Suit

It was rough country north of Pearcy, Ark., in 1938. My parents lived on an isolated slope of Pearcy Mountain, farming rented land. The house was built of rough lumber and the interior was unfinished. Two-by-four studs and the exterior plank siding were visible from the inside. We had no electricity, and an open fireplace provided heat in the winter. A well, which often dried up in midsummer, provided our water. The bathroom was an outhouse at the end of the footpath.

We kept a variety of animals on the farm—cows, horses, pigs, chickens, sheep, dogs and cats. I tried to make pets of them all. I was coming up on 4 years old that spring, and I figured I was approaching adult status.

My favorite pet was a sheep that was entitled to a small sample each time we milked the cows. I taught him to drink from the edge of a coffee can, like a person drinks from a glass. When I carried milk from the barn, I would pretend to forget that the sheep was waiting for

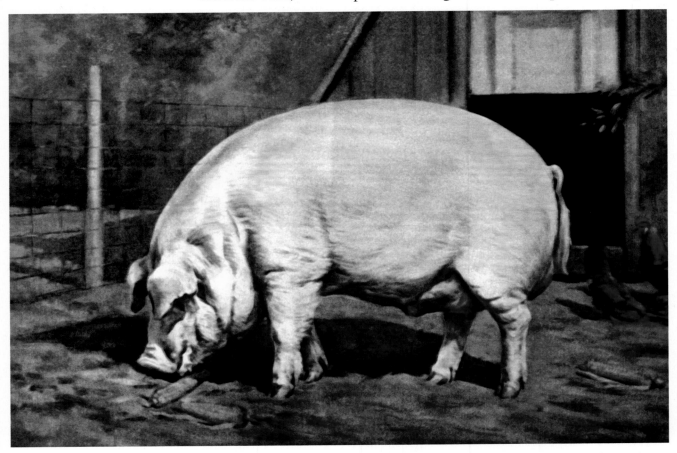

his treat. The poor animal would panic, retrieve his milk can, and chase me, bumping my leg with the can while bleating his message of hunger. When I reached the kitchen door, I relented and poured a cup of warm milk for the sheep.

I started making friends with the pigs before they were weaned, and one of them presumed to have as many privileges as the family dog. I named him Fat Boy. Too bad he was destined to end his career as pork chops. We allowed the pigs to roam the woods during the day, searching for acorns. Since we fed them at night, they never forgot to come home.

My father's most prized possessions were a pair of matched mules, John and Sam, named after two brothers-in-law. They weighed about 1,200 pounds each and worked well together.

He returned from plowing the fields one day, tired and bad-tempered. "Doyle, the well is almost dry. Take the mules to the spring and water them," he told me. "I'll take their harness off when you get back to the barn with them."

The mules towered over me, and the dust covering them was caked with sweat. They were tired from pulling the plow, and they were docile. The spring was about 600 yards into the forest, down a path, around the hill to a spot where water seeped from a sharp bluff and collected in a small pool. There was nothing but uninhabited forest beyond the spring, and I was a little afraid that a wandering mountain lion might consider me a good lunch.

The mules were easy to handle as I held the reins and drove them to the spring. But after they stood in the shade and drank their fill of the cool water, they started feeling frisky and were no longer inclined to take orders from a 40-pound boy. I gathered the reins and spoke crisply in my most commanding voice, "Gitty-up, mules. Haw, John." I pulled the reins to turn them toward the barn.

But the big animals had a different idea. They ignored me and bolted in the opposite direction, disappearing into the forest. I had to let go of the reins to avoid being dragged through the underbrush. I was scared as I watched them disappear. I knew my father would be furious with me for allowing the mules to escape, so I ran after them despite my fear of the forest. The mules ran through the brush, catching their harness on briars and branches and breaking a few straps. Then they circled the hill and returned to the barn, looking for someone to feed them.

They quickly outdistanced me, and I stopped, out of breath, lost and frightened. I wandered the hillside for what seemed an eternity, calling the mules and looking over my shoulder for some wild animal that might want to eat me.

I began to lose hope of finding my way home, and I started to cry.

As the sun sank lower, I began to lose hope of finding my way home, and I started to cry. The shadows were getting longer, and I imagined terrible creatures lurking in the woods after dark.

Then a familiar sound and a rustling noise just over the crest of a small hill arrested me. "Oink, oink," I heard, followed by the rustling of leaves being disturbed. "Oink, oink." Sure enough, Fat Boy was rooting contentedly through the leaves, eating acorns. I ran to him and tried to give him a hug. "Oink," he responded, turning from me to search for more acorns.

I was calm then and happily followed Fat Boy as he wandered through the forest, confident that I would be home for supper. Sure enough, as the sun sank behind the trees, Fat Boy picked up his pace and headed straight for home.

I followed him as he made a beeline for his pen and feeding trough. He had never missed feeding time, and that day was no exception.

My father was angry as he came out to confront me while I was letting Fat Boy into his pen. "Why didn't you hold onto those mules?" he demanded. "I ought to whip you. They've broken their harness, and it'll take me half a day to fix it."

But Mother interceded, pointing out that the two mules were about 60 times as heavy as I was, and perhaps it was unreasonable to expect me to control them.

Later, as I enjoyed supper, I was happy to be home safe, thankful to have avoided punishment, and plotting how I would keep control of those mules next time. ❖

The Little Red Mare

By Ralph Woodworth

Here is where it all started, my love affair with horses. Born just before the first World War, I was caught in the great infantile paralysis epidemic of that time, which killed and crippled so many children. Thank God, this disease—now called polio—has been eradicated by modern medicine.

There were many painful days in my early childhood, along with iron braces and operations. However, my most vivid recollection is of always being last to get where I was going. I remember wandering too far from home and having to make a slow and painful trip back.

House of White Birches nostalgia archives

We moved to a small suburban village in upstate New York when I was 7 or 8 years old. Here we had room for chickens, dogs—and a horse.

I had always been fascinated by horses. Many of them worked on the streets and farms nearby. I figured that if I had a horse, I could go as far and get back as quickly as anyone.

It took some time, but eventually my parents gave in and agreed to buy me a horse. First we tried two or three "used-up" horses cast off by our milkman and others. But they were so large that it was all but impossible for me to get on them.

Then, one day, my father saw a sign in a yard on his way home from work: "Pony for Sale." After supper, we went down to investigate. The pony turned out to be a Shetland mare not over 12 hands (48 inches) tall. A saddle, bridle and part of a driving harness came with her. The whole outfit cost $50.

My father was not a man to spend $50 lightly, but this looked like a worthwhile investment. At least it would shut me up and relieve him of horse hunting. Here was an animal small enough so I could get on her and cheap to care for, as ponies seldom need shoes and live mostly on grass or hay. My father paid the $50. One of my brothers led her the few blocks home.

Next day after school, I saddled the pony and rode her around the yard and up and down the sidewalks. Everything went fine. The following day, I repeated the performance, then staked her out. After supper, I decided to ride her again.

Now a problem arose; she refused to leave the yard. I would ride her as far as the street, and she would stop. I could ride up and down the drive as much as I wanted, but after supper, she would not leave the yard.

The next day after school, I climbed onto her and she went down the street without question. But again that evening after supper, she would not leave the yard.

Now I was beginning to hear stories around school about the pony a boy from the lower end of town had just sold. They said she had scared them by refusing to leave the barn and had thrown him off.

I put two and two together and figured out that they were talking about my little red pony. Within a few days, the story was all over school that I had got "stuck" with the outlaw pony.

Now, being crippled is not good for your disposition; it can make you a bit mean. But it can also give you determination, as things that are easy for most people can be very difficult for you. I remembered what my grandfather had told me. He was a coachman—never as respectable as the family would have liked, but he sure was a good horseman. Granddad said, "If you have horse trouble, don't set out to challenge him unless you really mean to do it. If you don't think you can win, don't start. Every time you get the job half done and then give up and let him beat you, it will be twice as hard to win the next battle."

That night after supper, I went out and saddled the pony. I got out the strap my father had fixed up with a loop so that I could carry it around the saddle horn. We started down the drive to the street, and as usual, we stopped.

I took the strap and "leathered her." She tried to buck. I had heard about this habit. I caught her a couple of good clouts across the nose with the strap, and that ended that.

I was getting pretty proud of myself and thought I had won the battle. But then she suddenly "folded up" and went down on her side and lay there. I got off, she got up; I got on, she lay down.

I could just hear the kids down at school snickering and saying that this pony had made a fool out of me. It was more than I could stand.

In our front yard was a pile of poles my father had trimmed off the trees to use for his pole beans. I grabbed one of those poles and brought it down across her ribs with a thump. At the same time, I applied my good foot to her rump. She was a very surprised pony. She leaped to her feet and almost got away from me.

I got on her, and she went down the street with no further problem.

The next night she went through the same performance. This time I gave her a few extra thumps. It was the last time I ever had a problem with her. The little red mare and I became the best of friends.

That little red mare was around for a long time. She was my legs.

I still heard snickers around school, so one afternoon after school, I hurried home and saddled up the little mare and rode her down behind the school where the kids were playing pick-up ball. I ran her around the yard and showed off what a good pony she was. The snickering stopped.

That little red mare was around for a long time. She was my legs. Before, when my father, sister and I had taken our Sunday-afternoon walks in the fields, they always had had to walk slowly so I could keep up. Now I could ride ahead and wait for *them.*

My father even fashioned a pair of shafts to fit my Flexible Flyer sled. In the winter, I spent many hours on that sled, bundled up in a blanket, behind the little mare.

Eventually I grew too big for the little mare and decided that it was time for a horse. I found a pretty black mare in a livery barn. But the dealer wanted $100 for her. My father had spent all he was going to spend on horses. He said if I could raise the money, I could have the horse.

This was a real problem. I figured my pony was worth $50. She had cost that amount, and in my mind, a $50 pony is a $50 pony as long as she lives.

As it turned out, fate was on my side. One evening, I was riding along the main road leading out of town. A big Pierce-Arrow touring car pulled up and stopped. It was one of those seven-passenger autos with extra seats in the rear that folded down into the floor when not in use.

A large, round-faced man got out and called me over. "Young man," he said, "would you sell that pony? I have been watching you ride and drive her around town, and I think she is just what I need for my grandson."

My grandfather's horse-dealing blood must have taken over. I suddenly saw visions of the black mare standing in our barn. I replied, "Yes, sir, I will take $100 for her, just as she is, with saddle and bridle." The big man looked like he could afford it.

He said, "That's a lot of money for a pony, but I'd pay it if I had some way to get her home." It was almost dark, and I knew that I couldn't ride her to the other side of town and get home before dark (my curfew). I was afraid to let him go home and think about it; tomorrow he might not be willing to pay $100.

Then an idea hit me. The mare would follow me anywhere I led her. "Sir," I said, "you just open the back door on that automobile, and I will put this pony in your backseat, and you can take her home right now."

With a surprised look, he replied, "Young man, if you can put that pony in that touring car, you will get your $100."

He opened both back doors. I took the reins and climbed in one door. Before I could get out the other, the little mare had jumped into the car just like a goat. I tied her to the blanket rail.

The big man handed me a $100 bill and I walked home. I had never seen $100 in any form, let alone in a single bill. The next day, I changed that $100 into the black mare that I had been hankerin' for.

I learned so much from that little red mare. She changed my life completely. She was my partner, my teacher and my legs. She gave me a love for small ponies that has lasted to this day.

Today, a child could not use a pony as I did 60 years ago. There is no place for them in town, and the dirt roads, riversides and wooded paths are no more. I am glad that I was born when such things were possible. ❖

Puppy Love

By Leone Dockstader

My husband was a veterinarian, and we bred and raised Boston terriers for 20 years. The puppies were so cute. We had a female, which we had bought as a puppy, named Dixie who had her first litter of just two puppies in June.

We had a building near the house in which we had several cages and a heating stove. But since Dixie had just two puppies, I brought her

box and puppies into the kitchen so I could care for them more easily. We had taken another female, soon to whelp, which the owner didn't want to keep. We put her in a cage in the barn.

I kept watch, and when I checked on her, I found she had five puppies. But she refused to accept them, pushing them into a corner, and she sat as far away from them as she could. This was very unusual.

After several attempts to get the mother to accept them, I decided I would have to bottle-feed them. I put the crying puppies in a box, and set them down on the kitchen floor while I got the nipples and bottles ready.

They were cold, hungry and crying. All at once, Dixie sat up, listened for a second, then jumped out of her box and went to the puppies' box. She cocked her head from side to side as if to say, "Are they my puppies? Where have they been?" Then she jumped in with them and got them to nurse.

Her own two were 10 days old by now. They were large, with eyes open, so I carried them out to the kennel and put them in a cage. I taught them to drink milk so that Dixie could take charge of the new little ones. This she did, and she raised all of them. Their own mother died that night. She had health problems, which was why she had refused to accept them. ❖

CCC Rescue

By Jenny Eden

In 1935, I was 5 years old. We lived in the small town of Caledonia in the southeastern corner of Minnesota. In those latter days of the Depression, there were breadlines at the bakery to buy day-old bread for a few pennies. Some of the churches set up soup kitchens to feed families that were having a rough time, but I don't remember ever being hungry. My mother always had a huge vegetable garden, and each of us kids had a small plot of our own to tend.

My father had a cleaning and tailoring shop, and he claimed that what really saved us was his idea for trade-in suits. Men would bring in their "like new" suits they had outgrown and trade them for something they could use. We survived on the few extra dollars.

President Roosevelt started WPA programs to keep young men working and food on their families' tables. A CCC camp was set up in the fairgrounds to house the young workers who worked on road projects. Some of the older people in our community were unhappy about this sudden influx of young men no one knew. All of my friends' parents instructed their kids to avoid contact with the strangers.

My mother had taken me with her to Father's shop that morning, as I was too young to go to school. But at noon, I ran home to check on my favorite kitty. Our beloved cat, Cinnamon, had produced four beautiful offspring. I picked up my favorite and carried her outside to see the snow.

She needed to touch the strange, fluffy stuff, so I put her down. Suddenly, the neighbor's dog appeared, and my terrified kitty fled up the nearest tree. My frightened screams only sent her higher.

A group of CCC men were working on a road crew down the street. One of them heard my cries and came running. I pointed up into the tree and kept crying. He smiled kindly at me. "Don't cry, little girl," he said. "I'll get her down for you."

He scaled that tree like he was born to it. But that little ball of fur saw the stranger as a further threat and climbed even higher. She was clinging to a very fragile branch when I heard it snap and saw her fall. The young man lunged, caught her in his gloved hand, tucked her inside his jacket and climbed down slowly and carefully.

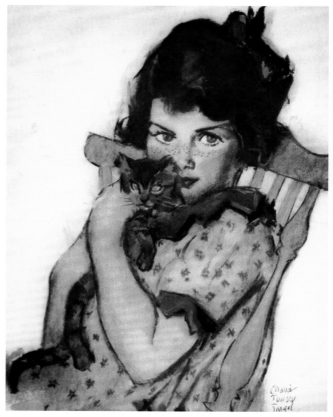

House of White Birches nostalgia archives

He grinned at me as he handed me my beloved pet. He had freckles, and a tooth was missing right in the middle of his wide grin. It was the most beautiful smile I had ever seen.

Mom invited him to dinner that night, and soon the whole town knew the story of his daring rescue. I can still see his face, and he will forever remain in my mind my handsome hero. ❖

Bounce

By Mary Haney

When I was a small child, we lived in the Ozarks, on a place called Deep Pond Ranch near the small town of Winona, Mo. We didn't have any nearby neighbors, so I didn't have anyone to play with, and at times, I was very lonely. My sister was 14 years older, so she was just another grown-up, not a playmate.

One day while I was playing in the front yard, a large brown dog came to the yard fence and lay down. He was thin and dirty, had burrs in his hair and cuts all over his body, and his feet were swollen, cut and bleeding. Daddy brought the dog in and laid him down on the front porch, giving him food and water. Then he started cleaning him up, cutting burrs out of his hair, doctoring his cuts with Black Salve (the best medicine that was ever invented—it could be used on anything). Then he cleaned, doctored and bandaged the dog's feet. The dog never flinched, growled, tried to bite or get away. He just seemed grateful to be cared for.

Mom said the good Lord had sent Bounce to be my guardian angel.

Daddy asked around, but no one knew of a missing dog fitting his description. I named the dog Bounce, and from that day on, he was my playmate and protector. Wherever I went, Bounce was by my side.

The countryside was still open range, and animals roamed wherever they wanted. One herd of horses was led by a big, mean stallion. No fence could keep him out. One day, as I was playing in the front yard with Bounce by my side, the horses came in sight. I ran up onto the front porch. The stallion jumped the fence, then came up onto the porch and started striking my little red wagon with his front hoof. Naturally, I was terrified and started screaming.

My mom jerked me into the house. Then Bounce flew into action, barking and nipping at the stallion's back legs until he got the horse off the porch and out of the yard and had chased the herd up the road. Then he came back to lie down beside me on the porch. Sometime after this incident, the stallion was found dead; someone had shot him.

Daddy had a sow that was gentle and easy to be around—until she had a litter of pigs. Then she became an old she-devil! One day I slipped away from Mom, and along with Bounce, went to see the baby pigs. The old sow saw me coming and started squealing and lunging against the fence, causing the top board to come loose.

Daddy had heard the noise and was running across the lot, but before he could get there, Bounce was already taking care of the problem. He had caught the sow by the nose, and he held her until Daddy could grab me and put me into the feed crib and fix the fence.

Once again, Bounce had protected me.

My sister, Doris, and I were walking down a path with Bounce by my side as always when suddenly, he got in the path right in front of us and started growling, his hair bristling. Doris tried to make him move, but there was no way he was going to let us go through, so she took me back to the house and told Daddy what was going on.

He took his gun and went to where Bounce was, and lo and behold, just beyond on the path lay a big copperhead snake. Daddy killed the snake. He said it was the biggest copperhead he had ever seen.

Our place had a big, deep pond, and I had been told to stay away from it. If I wandered off toward it, which Bounce knew I wasn't supposed to do, he'd try to get me to turn around. If that didn't work, he'd get me by my dress tail and pull me back to the house.

The day I started to school, Daddy had to tie Bounce to keep him from following me. But some time after we left, Bounce broke his chain and tried to follow anyway. He got as far as the highway, where he was struck and killed by a car. We found him when we came home that

evening. Daddy buried him under a tree in the front yard.

I've had other dogs through the years, but none was as special as Bounce. My mom always said the good Lord had sent Bounce to be my guardian angel, to keep an adventurous little girl from harm. Bounce was my friend and playmate.

Every child needs a dog like Bounce in their life. I am 63 years old, and I still have fond memories of my dog Bounce. ❖

Facing page: 1942 Prudential Insurance ad, courtesy Janice Tate

An Act of Friendship

By Lucy Sidbury

This is a true story, told to me by my mother about something unforgettable my grandfather did. When I was a little girl, my father and I always liked to go down to Benjamin Franklin Park to ice-skate. Almost every Saturday morning from December to March, we would get up early, eat a big breakfast and then, with our skates slung over our shoulders, walk the mile and a half to the park.

I always admired my dad and knew he was a kind and gentle person. But the events of one day in particular proved it forever.

It wasn't very cold on Saturday, even at 8 o'clock in the morning. It was March, and the sun was getting stronger all the time. But there had been a snowstorm the day before, so Dad and I thought that it would be a fine day for skating.

As usual, Rob Roy, our gentle, 7-year-old mixed-breed collie, trotted along beside us, carrying the stick he always took with him, as if to make up for not having ice skates. We ambled along the familiar city streets, looking in the store windows and nodding to people we knew, until finally, the fields and trees of the park came into view.

Rob Roy would bark and try to bite our skates and chase us on the pond.

No one else was around when we arrived. That made us happy, because that meant that we could do our tricks without being laughed at, and we could race each other from one end of the pond to the other.

How good it felt to have the wind at my back and the cold, clear air on my face. I would push my skates as hard as I could to pick up speed and then glide smoothly, sometimes skating backward, sometimes doing figure eights or little jumps—and, many times, falling.

Rob Roy would bark and try to bite our skates and chase us around the pond, but he soon learned that paws were useless on ice.

When Dad chased me, I laughed so hard I couldn't keep up the strength to escape. When he finally caught me, I hugged him hard and thought about how much I loved him.

We were having such fun when suddenly I heard a crack and a splash! I looked in the direction of the sound, but I couldn't see anything. Then my dad raced past me to the far side of the pond and stopped by a small, jagged hole in the ice. Rob Roy had gone to the other side of the pond—the sunny side—to investigate something, and the softening ice had given way beneath him.

I hurried across to help, but Dad shouted, "Stay back!"

My heart pounded with fear as I looked for the dog. Then his head appeared through the hole. With great difficulty, he tried to keep his head above the ice.

It was about 50 feet from the hole to the side of the pond—not too far to swim under normal circumstances, but the ice was too thick for the dog to break through.

"What can we do?" I screamed. Then I started to crawl to Rob.

"Get off the ice!" my father yelled. "We'll get him out." I had heard of dogs saving people many times, but what I witnessed next, in my mind, would repay that debt forever.

My father threw off his winter coat and removed his ice skates. Then he ran to the edge of the pond closest to the dog. Before my startled eyes, he hurled himself onto the ice, breaking it and plunging into the freezing water. Again and again, my father threw himself down, and then pounded the ice with his fists.

"Hold on, old Rob! Just a minute, boy, and I'll have you out of there! I'll get you, lad!" my father shouted frantically. The dog responded to his encouragement and kept struggling.

I could hardly believe my father's strength of body and spirit. I wondered about Rob's strength, fearing he would soon go under.

Twenty feet, 10—Dad could almost touch the freezing, frightened animal. Now my father's teeth were chattering, as time after time, he sank up to his neck in the water. Chunks of ice lay behind him as he carved a path to Rob Roy. Then, after what seemed like hours, he broke through.

Treading water, my dad patted Rob's head and then slowly pushed the dog ahead of him until both man and beast lay on the bank. My dad, soaked to the skin in his heavy, wet clothing, gasped for air.

Rob Roy shook himself and walked over to Dad. Whimpering, he licked his face. "All right now, boy. It's all right," my father whispered. I hugged Rob and kissed my father and thanked God a thousand times that they were alive.

We slowly started to walk home, but as the March wind blew around my father's wet form, we decided that it would be better to run. We had a mile and a half to go, and I am still amazed that he could do it. But getting home quickly saved my father from serious illness.

When we finally reached our house, we fell, gasping, into the hallway. My mother was surprised to see us back so soon, and then horrified by the sight of my father's wet clothes. She made him go right upstairs to take a hot bath. Then she questioned me about what had happened.

As I was telling the story, Rob Roy disappeared. We wanted to dry him thoroughly and give him a bowl of warm milk. We searched the kitchen, dining room—everywhere downstairs, calling repeatedly. Then we went upstairs, and there he was, lying in front of the bathroom door, waiting for Dad.

When my father left the bathroom and went into his bedroom, Rob followed him. He lay by Dad's bed all night. The next morning, the dog would not let my father out of his sight.

In the past, Rob had always stayed around me and had not paid too much attention to my father. But from that day until he died, Rob Roy was Dad's dog. He never forgot who had saved his life.

It has been a long time since that cold March day, but whenever the conversation turns to friendships, childhood, or our beloved Rob Roy, I am reminded of a quote from the Bible: "There is no greater love than this, to lay down one's life for one's friends." ❖

The Dog

By Nick Kenny

A faithful dog will play with you,
And laugh with you, or cry.
He'll gladly starve to stay with you,
And never reason why.

If you are feeling out of sorts,
Somehow, he'll understand.
He'll watch you with his shining eyes
And try to lick your hand.

His blind, implicit faith in you
Is matched by his great love—
The kind that all of us should have,
In the Master, up above!

When everything is said and done,
I guess this isn't very odd,
For when you spell "dog" backward,
You get the name of "God."

No Way Out

By Romaine Mann

My aunt was visiting us for a few days and making clothes for my new, 18-inch, double-jointed doll. I thought about my new dolly and her new clothes all day. When school let out that afternoon, I told the other kids going my way that I had to go to the privy—they were just to go on, and I would catch up with them. But then I thought I would cross the fields to save time, so I started to walk until I came to the east rim of the ravine.

In 1908, when I was 7, I lived on a farm close to Round Top Mountain south of Middletown, Pa. There had just been a 20-inch snow, and the day after was blizzardy, with bad drifts. I went to a one-room school at New Berry at the foot of the mountain, four fields from my home. We wore felt boots to school, which enabled us to walk on the crust of the snow.

A 21-foot ravine ran right down from the mountain to Swatara Creek. The afternoon sun had partially melted the crust, and all at once, I started to slide down to the bottom of the ravine, at the bottom of which was a mountain stream about 4 feet wide and 6 inches deep. I crossed it, jumping from stone to stone, then came to an old chestnut

Rose ran right over to the edge of the ravine and barked down at me.

tree that had three trunks. This was kind of familiar, for we had similar trees close to the school grounds, and we used to play in between the trunks. Putting moss in for carpet and little stones for walks, we spent many happy hours there—so I climbed up and sat right in among the three trunks.

Then, about 4 feet farther up, was a stump, so I grabbed some branches and climbed up to sit there. I fell off backward, though, and slid down to the stream. Luckily, only one leg got in the water. Now I had snow down my neck and one wet foot, so I climbed into the chestnut tree against, took my stocking off to wring the water out, then put it back on under my felt boot.

I started to talk to myself. *No way out … the ravine runs from the mountain to the creek. I will call Papa.*

So I started calling, and the echo from the mountain called back: *Pa-pa-pa-pa.* I got scared, for I did not know it was an echo. I thought someone else was calling too, so I did not call again.

When my legs got stiff from sitting all hunched up, I'd stand for a while. I could faintly hear our dog barking back in the yard, and then, all at once, a beautiful red fox came running down the east rim from the mountain. It never turned its head, but went lickety-split with its big, bushy tail hanging on behind.

By now the sky was getting gray, and there were eerie shadows of trees and rocks on the east side of the ravine. I thought I saw a man sitting on a rock and writing in the snow.

My teacher had given me a big seed catalog to give to my father. I laid it on the snow, unbuttoned the cape from my coat, and laid it on the catalog to sit on. My felt boots were beginning to warm my feet again. I kept watching what I thought was a man, and soon I went to sleep.

Later, I woke to our dog, Rose, barking in the distance. I saw two lanterns and heard *crunch, crunch* in the snow. After a bit, I heard my name called. Rose was barking right up in my father's face. I screamed, "Here I am, Rose! Down here!" Rose ran right over to the edge of the ravine and barked right down at me.

Dad put a rope around Clarence, our hired man, and let him down. Clarence put the rope around me, and my dad pulled me up and then Clarence. Rose was so happy to see me that she twisted like a fish worm. She always did this when she was happy.

I opened my dinner basket and gave her the egg sandwich I hadn't eaten for lunch, for I had been given a pork chop and jelly bread. I walked home with Dad and Clarence, hand in hand.

When we got home, Mom put me beside the open oven door and gave me a teaspoonful of whiskey and sugar in a cup of hot water as my feet thawed in warm water.

I played with my doll for a while, then ate a supper of ham and *snitz* and *knept*. Then she covered me up in bed with my feather tick.

The next morning, I asked my father how he knew I was in the ravine. He said Rose knew. ❖

The Bays or the Baby

By Ruth Dirck

My dad and his sister, Mae, were having a difficult time hitching the new, high-spirited racing team. The gleaming red racing cart just must not be scratched! Actually, it was too cold to be driving on that January day in 1902, but Daddy couldn't wait to show off his beautiful bays to the lovely girl he was going to marry. My mother was the only daughter of a doctor who lived several miles away in the country village of Dunksburg, Mo.

As Daddy arrived at her home, a young couple with a sick baby drove up to the doctor's office and rushed inside. Meanwhile, Mama came out to see the beautiful matched pair of bays that were snorting and pawing the snow. A few minutes later, her father called Daddy into his office. Mama held the bays and soothed them, though she was uneasy at their high spirits.

The doctor told Daddy that the baby the couple brought in was dying and he had no way of saving her. He said Dr. Patterson in Warrensburg had some new equipment that might save her. However, the baby must be taken there quickly or it would be too late. Daddy thought of his new team as the young mother sobbed. He said, "I'll have them at the train station as fast as I can."

The doctor shook his head. "The train going west will be too late."

"All right," Daddy answered. "I'll take them to Warrensburg." He looked at the young father, who was a big man. His racing cart only held two people. "Let your wife take the baby. Your weight would slow the horses and cramp my driving," he said.

In seconds they were off. Daddy held the bays to a fast trot. They had 28 miles of snow-covered roads to travel. The doctor ran to the telegraph office to send a wire to Dr. Patterson.

The miles flew by under the horses' long strides. Daddy glanced at the blanket-wrapped mother. She was only a girl, really. She was not crying now, but her lips moved as she prayed.

A mile or so from the station, she said, "I think she is gone." Daddy slowed the horses for a much-needed rest. He gently lifted the blankets to look at the little face. As the frigid air reached her, the little one gasped, then weakly cried.

"Thank you, God; she is still alive," Daddy prayed. Then he spoke to his horses, urging them into a dead run. As they flew past the depot, the telegrapher waved an arm of encouragement. He had relayed the doctor's message. Now he rushed back in to tap out a second one.

On and on the horses ran. They were white with frosty foam now. Their expert driver urged them on, guiding them surely over the hills. Daddy glanced at the mother. Her face was blue with cold. Her long eyelashes closed with ice. "Shall we stop and warm up at bit at a farmhouse?" Daddy asked.

She shook her head. "No! No! The baby is still breathing. She is still alive!" Daddy's own face was numb with cold. He knew his horses might not stand this killing pace for many more miles, but he would try. He drove with one hand, trying to warm the other under his arm. If his hands stiffened, it would hinder his driving.

Warrensburg came into view. The left bay stumbled, but Daddy's quick lift of the rein helped him recover his footing. They sped on. "Thank you, God, for this cart," Daddy whispered. "The wheels would have gone miles back on anything else."

The last mile was pure torture for the laboring, sweating horses, but at last they swung into the lane leading to Dr. Patterson's home office. The doctor ran out, picked up the mother and baby in his arms and ran for the house. "I'll save these two!" he called out to Daddy. "You save those two horses!"

Slowly, he painfully drove his precious racers a few more blocks to the livery stable. All hands and the owner came out. They broke the ice from buckles and straps, pleading with Daddy to go warm himself. but he helped with the bays until each was rubbed and blanketed. Boys began walking them up and down the runway.

Then he dropped into a chair by the big-bellied stove in the office. The trembling began. The owner of the livery stable was Lark Blackburn, a handsome man near Daddy's age. He

brought Daddy a steaming mug of beef broth, steadying his shaking hands with his own strong ones as Daddy drank. Then, reaching for a glass on the desk, Lark poured straight whiskey to the brim. The whiskey followed the broth and soon the shaking stopped. Immediately Daddy went back to his horses.

Lark left them to go to the doctor's home. He returned with good news. The baby was responding to treatment with the new equipment, and she would be all right. The mother had been warmed, fed and put to bed. Had they arrived 10 minutes later, the baby could not have lived.

Everyone congratulated Daddy! He was glad and thankful that the baby would live, but he did not feel much like a hero as he worked to save his horses.

They heard the westbound train whistle as it came into Warrensburg. A few minutes later, Aunt Mae came flying into the livery stable. She had ridden to the station in time to catch the train. Now, peeling off her lovely coat, tossing her fur muff onto a chair and catching a man's jacket from the floor, she was ready to help with the horses. Daddy, Aunt Mae and Lark Blackburn worked all night. As day began to dawn, they knew that the two beautiful horses would live. But they could never race again. Light driving would be all their hearts could stand.

Years later, my dad pointed out a young lady to me. As only he would put it, he said, "I took that doll for a buggy ride when she was a baby." ❖

> *"I'll save these two!" the doctor called out to Daddy. "You save those two horses!"*

My Dog, Dido

By Charley Sampsell

My first pet was a large, long-haired white cat named Esau. I don't know how he came to live at our small southwestern Michigan farm. Perhaps he was born there, though we had no other white cats. Or, more likely, he was abandoned near our house by someone blessed with an unexpected litter of kittens.

When I was about 3 years old, in 1928, my mother took a picture of me with Esau and entered it in a contest for best photos of farm children. To enhance our chances of winning, she took the liberty of changing Esau's name to Puff when submitting the picture. She was very happy when the picture was published in a farm magazine to which we subscribed. She was even more elated when she received $3 prize money. Cash was a rare commodity at our house in those days. I'm not sure how long we enjoyed Esau's company, but by the time I was old enough to remember things clearly, he was gone.

We supported a half-dozen or so assorted cats around our barn to help control the mouse and rodent population. They were not pets or house cats, but they were fed twice a day in the barn and generally considered that building their home. They only came to the house once or twice a day to find out why nobody was getting serious about milking the cows and giving them their rations.

I wanted to stay longer and play with my new best friend.

My dad was a dedicated rabbit hunter and therefore always had one or two beagle hounds around to assist him. They were friendly and playful, but prone to disappearing for long periods whenever they were not chained to their houses.

None of these animals exactly fit the job description of a young boy's playmate. I was 8 years old in 1933 when that position was finally filled satisfactorily.

My cousin, Pearl, was considerably older than I was. She was married and lived on a farm near Lansing, Mich. My mother and I visited her one fine spring day, and while the ladies were talking and touring the garden and other points of interest on the farm, I was allowed to play with a litter of pups that were only a few weeks old.

One of them was a roly-poly little bundle of black-and-white fur that seemed to take an instant liking to me. Soon he was following me all around the yard, barking and tugging at the cuffs of my jeans.

By the time Mom and Cousin Pearl returned, we were literally inseparable. He wouldn't let go of my sock. It was time for us to go,

Facing page: 1932 *The Country Home*, House of White Birches nostalgia archives

but I didn't want to leave. I wanted to stay longer and play with my new best friend.

My dear cousin sensed the strength of our bonding. Though the dogs were purebred American Kennel Club–registered English springer spaniels, worth a fairly substantial sum, she told Mom that I could have the pup of my choice.

My selection was already determined, and soon we were in our Model T Ford, motoring the 75 miles back to our farm at Portage Lake. Mom was a little concerned about my dad's reaction to a bird dog in addition to his hounds, but I was in a state of pure euphoria.

If Dad had any objection, he and Mom must have worked it out, for I heard no protest. I was simply advised that the care of the new member of the family would be my responsibility. We were together 24 hours a day, and within a few weeks, we were able to communicate and understand each other with very few words required.

Soon the problem of a name had to be faced. He already had a three- or four-word official name on his registration papers, but that was useless for everyday purposes. I noticed that on Mom's baking days, the puppy loved to eat scraps of leftover raw dough. For several weeks we called him Do-Do (rhyming with "dough-dough").

Somehow, however, that appellation just didn't seem to fit a high-spirited, fun-loving dog. Dad had a favorite expression for active playfulness, "cutting didoes." Soon Do-Do evolved into Dido, and that was his name for the rest of his life.

During the next several years, Dido grew to middle age and I became a teenager. Together we learned to hunt, fish and swim, to wander into and out of Portage Lake and the Portage

Dido and the author in 1937.

River, to eat wild berries and fruit where we found them as we wandered through woods and fields, to run through summer cornfields until we were ready to drop, and then to flop down onto deep grass under a tree and snooze until we regained our energy. It was a great time for both of us, and we were seldom apart for long.

On a fine July day in 1937, when I was 12 years old, I put on my swim trunks under my jeans and Dido and I took off across fields to the home of my two best friends, Dick and Len. The three of us and Dido then set out to explore the Portage River for about a half mile down to the village of Parkville.

The river probably averaged a foot deep in that stretch, but there were places where it was only a few inches deep and other spots where the depth was 6–8 feet.

At Parkville there was a dam and a spillway from an old gristmill. When we reached the millrace, Len, who was my age and about my size, and I debated whether or not we had the nerve to swim across the deep hole, which was about 20 feet wide. After several rounds of "I dare you" and "You're yellow," we found ourselves paddling strongly across the race. Brother Dick, who was a year older, 6 inches taller and considerably smarter, remained on the bank, watching.

All went well until we were about halfway across. Then we encountered a much stronger current and a swirling whirlpool, which seemed to hold us firmly in its grasp no matter how hard we paddled.

Len's arms gave out first and he went under with a weakly gasped "Help!" Before he came up, I, too, ran out of steam and silently submerged while inhaling half a lungful of water. When I came up, I saw Len just going down for the second time, Dick jumping into the water and heading toward him, and Dido on the bank, barking wildly and looking confused. Then I did my second unintended dive, this time grabbing a quick half-breath before it was too late.

My next return to the surface revealed Dick up to his eyes in the water, dragging Len by the hair toward the shore, and Dido right in front of me, paddling furiously and looking for me. In desperation, I grabbed him by the collar and pushed him under long enough to gasp in another bit of air. Dido never stopped paddling. While I was still under water, he managed to move us a step or two toward the shore, where my wildly reaching tiptoes gained purchase on the river bottom and propelled me into chin-deep water.

That was my first encounter with a life-threatening situation, and the scare it gave me was a great caution-builder. Needless to say, I made no mention of the fiasco at home that evening. Some things are better left untold. Mom and Dad might have wondered why I was so solicitous of Dido's comfort and well-being that night.

Dido lived for several more years, during which we were separated more frequently than I liked. In 1945, when he was 13, I returned home on furlough from the Air Force during pheasant-hunting season in Michigan. One evening, we went out for a short hunt in the hayfield on our farm next to Portage Lake. Dido was no longer able to run swiftly back and forth about 30 yards in front of me as a good spaniel should. He could only manage to keep the proper distance in front and work a few feet to either side. Still, he was able to flush a fine cock, which we bagged.

A few weeks after I had returned to duty, Mom wrote me a letter: "I have bad news. Yesterday we had to take Dido over to Doc Gorsline's and have him put to sleep. We couldn't stand to see him in so much pain." I left the barracks and went for a walk while I shed some tears over the loss of a wonderful friend.

Fifty-some-odd years later, whenever I see a black-and-white springer spaniel walking with its owner, I still feel a pang or two and entertain fond memories of my dog, Dido. ❖

A True Friend

By Letha Fuller

We moved from Buffalo, N.Y., to a cozy cottage with five acres of land across from the Genesee River in the village of Scio, N.Y. Here at last we were able to have a pet for the children.

Impy was a pure white puppy, part terrier and part Spitz. She was full of mischief and fun, and we all loved her dearly. She soon learned she should never go near the road. Daily, when the school bus was due, she ran to the end of the porch and waited there with her paws on the railing, ready to greet Jack and Jean.

Impy made friends with our large white rabbit, Mitz. They chased each other in the snow. Sometimes they even napped together.

One day we were returning from a shopping trip in Wellsville. As we neared our home, we saw a line of stopped cars.

Frank got out of the car to investigate. In the middle of the road in front of our house sat Mitz, our rabbit. Impy was barking frantically as she ran in circles around the rabbit to protect her from the cars.

People in their cars watched patiently as Frank hurriedly picked up the frightened rabbit, waved the traffic on and walked into the yard with Impy jumping excitedly after him.

Impy received an extra bone, and Mitz was returned to her wire cage. Would a dog risk her life to save a friend? ❖

Impy, the author's pet and friend.

Dad's Friend, Smoky

By Clyde Richards

My dad walked the same mail route for 32 years. Dedicated completely to the post office, my father earned a host of friends during his long years of service. But none was more loyal or dependable than the lumbering half-breed St. Bernard named Smoky. For a handful of years, the fawn-colored dog knew every foot of the residential route. He intimidated other dogs by his sheer size, and yet he exhibited a placid and gentle nature to all he met, especially children.

None could resist the sometimes-sad reflection in his brown eyes or the understanding cant of his massive head.

Smoky lived on one of the first streets on Dad's route, and he lumbered off the porch, wagging his bushy tail, before my father reached the comfortable, Grove Street home.

An excellent companion, the big dog stayed close, sniffing here and there, but never far. He often traversed the entire route with Dad, but some days he returned to his familiar porch after only a few streets.

Years before mail carriers delivered by vehicle, they withered under summer heat and endured harsh Maine winters. Smoky panted and slowed his pace in the turgid heat and limited his companionship during the hottest days of summer.

Throughout his rescue, Smoky never relaxed his grip on his bone

But he stayed with Dad throughout the worst days of winter, unaffected by heavy snows, blizzards and the deep cold accelerated by fierce winds from the northwest. Plodding along during snowstorms, the dog resembled an energetic snowman!

Known to virtually everyone in our small town, Smoky enjoyed a dog's life and exhibited few faults. He might chase a cat or two (he was surprisingly quick and agile for his size) or deliver a deep-throated growl toward any other canine that challenged his step with my father, but he was not a fighter.

His family appreciated him turning away peddlers and door-to-door salespeople with a baleful glare and rumbling growl. A singular fall from grace occurred when the big dog was accused of killing a bull terrier at a time when he was not accompanying Dad on the mail route. Maybe yes and perhaps no; the facts were never clear.

The big brute took part in an occasional adventure with his usual calm demeanor, reflecting one of the many reasons he was so graciously accepted by people of the community. But one event on a quiet street shattered his placid nature, at least for a few moments.

Two spinster sisters who ran a millinery shop on Main Street lived in a well-ordered brown bungalow on Dad's route. One morning, my father stepped onto their porch and was followed by the sisters' coon cat. The kitty streaked through a hinged door near the bottom of the screen.

Never one to ignore a fleeing cat, Smoky pounded up the steps and onto the porch after the scrambling feline. Smoky also went through the screen door—taking the lower sash and screening into the house with him!

One of the sisters happened to be home at the moment. One can only imagine her consternation at the sight of the tawny beast chasing her prized cat into the house.

Dad yelled and berated the big pooch until Smoky hunkered at the edge of the lawn, crestfallen and not understanding Dad's wrath. The lady of the house, assured that her kitty had come through the affair unscathed, refused to let Dad make amends by paying for the shattered screen door, and their trek along the route resumed.

Smoky could never catch an agile cat, but he darned well proved he knew how to scramble through a screen door after one.

Smoky attained a measure of local notoriety as an indirect result of my father's generosity. During the winter, Dad occasionally procured a bone from Peter Vincent's IGA store for his canine pal.

One late-winter day, Smoky accepted his treat, wagged his tail and trotted home, taking a shortcut down behind the store, over the railroad tracks and across the frozen surface of Lake Wassookeag's lower end.

At the time of this misadventure, another spring was manifesting itself by infrequent warm sun, muddy driveways and the start of the breakup of winter ice on Lake Wassookeag. With the large bone in his jaws, Smoky trotted toward the lake.

The author's father, Wes Richards, with Smoky at the author's family home in Dexter, Maine, in July 1943.

Perhaps in his anxiety to reach home and chomp the large bone, the big dog apparently failed to notice the dark and porous nature of the ice and the pools of water that accented the melting. When he was almost halfway across the sagging, buckling surface, the ice gave way, and Smoky found himself in frigid water, frantically paddling.

The dog's plight attracted customers entering the store, and Peter Vincent called Fred Keyte, a coal dealer down the street. Keyte, an officer of the volunteer fire department, and another fireman, Pat Pooler, drove the old Essex hook-and-ladder truck down behind the IGA store and stretched the longest ladder onto the ice.

Crawling on the sagging ladder and soaked by icy, seeping water, they reached Smoky and together grasped his collar. Struggling mightily, they persisted in their efforts to free the burly animal from his watery prison. Once retrieved, he warily made his way to his own back yard. All throughout his ordeal and his rescue, Smoky never relaxed his grip on the bone.

The news about everybody's friendly dog and his escape from the cold waters of Wassookeag spread around the town in the next few days. My father, who had proceeded along his route after giving Smoky the bone, did not hear of the dog's affair until the next day.

The next time they procured a bone at the IGA store, Dad's loyal companion did not attempt to cross the ice-covered end of the lake. In fact, residents near the lake did not remember ever seeing the big pooch cross the ice again.

I've always believe that through my father's 32 years walking a mail route, some of his happiest days were those when a big dog trotted beside him. ❖

Nikki's Gift

By Bob Johnson

Since last January, my 85-year-old mother has resided in a nursing home. While the nursing home is a clean, well-staffed facility, many of the elderly inhabitants take little notice of life around them. They sit slumped in wheelchairs in hallways, nearly oblivious to the continuous parade of workers and visitors walking past them. To me, these people appear more dead than alive.

On our most recent visit to Mother, our small, mixed-breed terrier, Nikki, made the 300-mile trip with my wife and me. After we'd spent an hour visiting with Mother, I excused myself to return to my minivan to "water" Nikki. Leaving Mother's room, I made my way past the dozing, laconic wheelchair patients. As usual, the old folks showed no sign of recognition or interest. *Is this the way we'll be at the end*? I mused.

After Nikki "powdered her nose," I decided to sneak her inside the nursing home. Mother hadn't seen our dog for a long time. No one stopped me downstairs as I entered carrying Nikki.

When we exited the second-floor elevator, a frail-looking man who was slouched in a wheelchair slowly raised his head.

> *"Had dogs all my life. Loved every one of 'em," the old man said.*

Straightening up, his weathered face wrinkled into a grin. "Doggie, doggie," he said, reaching out a gnarled hand. "What's his name?"

"Nikki. She's a girl," I said as I lifted the dog closer so that he could touch her. The old man gently moved his misshapen fingers through Nikki's soft fur. Delighted with all the attention, Nikki's tail beat wildly.

"Had dogs all my life. Loved every one of 'em," the old man said.

"Dogs are wonderful," I agreed.

"Yes, they're God's creatures. Nice meeting you, Nikki."

The dog and I continued to walk toward Mother's room. As we approached the dozing wheelchair patients, nearly every one of them became alert.

Only moments ago, these same people had seemed to be in a deathlike trance. Now they smiled, and their hands reached out to touch the dog. I held her close so they all could touch her. Excited, Nikki's tail thumped a mile a minute.

Finally we reached Mother's room. After a loud bark hello, Nikki jumped up on the bed and greeted Mother.

"Who owns that animal?" a loud, New England–accented voice said from the doorway.

"We do," I said defensively. "I'll take her outside. My mother hasn't seen Nikki for a long time."

"Oh, it's all right," the nurse responded. "We allow dogs to visit. There are a couple of bed-riddens down the hall who'd like to meet your dog. Would you mind?"

"No, of course not," I said.

The nurse led the way to a private room near Mother's. An old woman, looking terribly sick and frail, was propped up in the bed. Her old face seemed to come to life when she saw Nikki.

I watched as she tenderly stroked the dog. After a brief visit, she was visibly energized.

We entered the rooms of three other bedridden residents. Their happy, animated reactions were much the same as the first woman's. Just the simple act of touching my little dog seemed to bring them back to life. When we returned to Mother's room, the nurse said, "It's amazing how seeing a cat or dog perks these folks up."

"I guess animals kindle wonderful memories. If we didn't live six hours away, I'd bring Nikki with us every time we visit. The trip's brutal on her bladder," I said.

"Well, bring her back if you can," the nurse said. "Our patients love her."

A little later, Mother had grown tired, and we rose to leave. I held Nikki so that Mother could kiss the dog's head, and I watched as the old woman received a wet tongue on her cheek.

As we strolled toward the elevator, many of the slumped-over patients reawakened. Once again, I held Nikki close to every hand that wanted to touch her. Nearly all the hands reached out.

"Come and see me again," several old people said as we passed.

As we drove out of the nursing home's parking lot, I pledged that Nikki would accompany us on all future visits. And for the very first time since Mother had been ambulanced to this facility, I drove away without tears in my eyes. ❖

Editor's Note: Recent research has borne out the author's observations. The use of pets (such as the dog in the photograph at right) to reach out to the elderly in nursing homes and extended care facilities has become a common way that pets continue to come to the rescue.

The Cat's Meow

Chapter Three

Maybe it's true. Maybe sharing your life with a pet really *can* increase life expectancy up to seven years. I don't know if there is any scientific evidence to support that recent claim in the news. But I think my love of cats has certainly made my life more complete through the years.

The first pet Janice and I had was Beans, a mongrel kitten that showed up on our door step one day. We can't remember why we called her Beans. Pinto beans and cornbread were staples for dinner and supper back then, so maybe the cat's name came from that.

I never got tired of beans or Beans.

Beans was a wonderful cat who traveled with us all over the United States. Janice taught her to walk on a leash because we were afraid she would disappear while we were picking apples as itinerant workers in Washington state.

Beans was the first in a long line of feline friends through all these decades. Fluffy was a long-haired cat that we found raiding garbage cans near our home in southern California back in the early 1970s. She had no collar and obviously was abandoned. The first sighting pulled at our heartstrings. By the time we saw her the third and fourth times, we knew we had to do something. So, Fluffy came home with us.

Our next cat was a Lone Star native. Cocoa was a slick-haired male, once again a vagrant who came and adopted our family while we were living in Texas. Cocoa saw our children grow up, and then moved with us as we returned to the old home place in the Ozark Mountains.

When we moved, Cocoa rode back in the cab of the moving truck we rented. As soon as the door opened upon our arrival, Cocoa shot out of the cab like a bullet. After weeks we came to the heavy-hearted decision that he was gone forever.

Four months later, Cocoa showed up with a "who is this interloper" attitude toward Sunshine, the stray we had adopted in the interim. Cocoa had spent the time at a farm three miles down our country lane.

I guess he finally came home only when he was good and ready.

Another 20 years have passed. Cocoa and Sunshine, like Beans and Fluffy, are now gone.

Today Buster, Scamper and Bebe are now the companions who are increasing our life expectancy. Buster is a scaredy-cat who runs at the first hint of trouble. Scamper was abandoned by her mother as a too-small kitten and then nursed to health by Janice and her trusty eyedropper. Scamper still thinks Janice is her mother and is most content curled up along Janice's side in bed.

Bebe is fully my cat. She awakens me in the morning with her insistent cry to come turn on the water in the bathroom sink so she can get a drink. Bebe drink from the same dish as the other two cats? That would be undignified. At times I find myself walking about our home busy with menial tasks, almost forgetting that Bebe is snuggled in the crook of my arm.

The stories in this chapter remind me of how our cats moved into our homes and then into our hearts. I don't know if they increased our life expectancy, but they enriched our lives beyond measure. These memories, like our feline friends, are the cat's meow.

—*Ken Tate*

> *Our cats moved into our homes and then into our hearts.*

JOHN FALTER

The Unfathomable House Cat

By Rodney C. Peabody

Of all the creatures that roam the earth, I believe the ordinary house cat is head and whiskers above all the other tribes, including mankind. It is impossible to describe the house cat with precise characteristics as a group, or tribe, or strain, or breed, as you can describe most all other species on this planet. All of the 30 or 40 house cats I have known down through the years have had similar characteristics. But each had the most independent, unpredictable and unique personality all its own.

They seem to look at the rest of the world with haughty superiority and disdain. They apparently feel that the whole world was created just for them. They believe it their right to roam at will and choose this home or that home and then dominate the whole household. Everything revolves around the cat and its whimsical notions.

We—Mom, Dad, Janice and I—were blessed with our first cat in 1925 when I was 6 years old. A little tiger, about one-third grown, turned up one day and stayed around for a couple of days. Sis and I started sneaking food out to it and finally told Mom and asked if we could keep it.

> *My brothers were watching Father fill a cooled thermos with lemonade.*

Well, as usual with moms, she had realized that this crisis was coming. She and Dad had already decided that we could keep it, as we had never had a pet of any kind before. It was a beautifully formed and colored tiger cat—black and gray, with an exceptional head and face and long tiger-striped tail, which she used to communicate her mood, attitude, and mental reactions, as most cats do.

The next problem was a name. And that can be a big problem with four people trying to agree. But Sis and I won out. We called it Andy, after Andy Gump in the funny paper. We made a big mistake, of course. But as I was 6 and Janice was 10, we didn't give a thought as to the sex of the kitten. We liked the name Andy, so that's what her name became.

Dad would get down on the floor and make a sort of tent out of the newspaper. Then he would take his long, yellow pencil and play with Andy as she tried to get the pencil under the newspaper.

She would try all sorts of tricks and tactics. She'd sneak up very slowly, or she'd give a kind of growl and jump with all four feet right in the middle of the paper; but Dad would have the pencil sticking out an inch or two at one edge, and she'd pounce in that direction, only to miss.

Janice and I thought it was hilarious to see our big ol' Dad down on the floor, playing with a cat. He played that way with every cat we ever had, and so did Sis and I, even after we were grown and married with our own kids. We would play with our cats with a newspaper and pencil just as Dad had done.

In December 1925, we moved from Elyria, Ohio, to a little town (population 1,200) in Indiana. Dad had done a lot of free-lance writing while working as a surveyor on the New York Central Railroad. When he was offered a job as associate editor of *Specialty Salesman Magazine* in South Whitley, Ind., we moved, lock, stock, and barrel. Andy came with us, too, to what we kids thought was a land infested with Indians and bears, being way out west of Ohio!

We worried about Andy because she was in a cage in the baggage car and we knew she was scared. But she made the trip as well as we did.

Dad had rented one of the larger, nicer homes in town. It had a big, wide porch running halfway around the house; it was a perfect place to play in rainy weather.

Andy took over the new house just as if she had picked it out and made all the arrangements, paid the rent, etc. She was in charge of everything.

A few months after we arrived in South Whitley, Mom went to get the dirty clothes basket out of my closet, and there was Andy curled up in it—and she was not alone.

There were five or six tiny kittens snuggled up against her. Mom called Sis and me to come upstairs and see what she had found. We did, and boy, were we thrilled. Her first kittens! (Sis and I realized then that we had made a mistake with her name.)

But, what the heck, she was still Andy, kittens and all. Andy gave us several more kittens before she died of old age. But she sure had a good life.

The only other cat that really matched Andy in our affections was a big yellow tiger, tough as nails, a tomcat. And he was a fighter.

I was at eighth-grade basketball practice one evening after school when one of the kids said that his grandma, who lived across the street from the gym, had a bunch of kittens, and "Let's go see them."

So we did, and she had four of the prettiest yellow-and-white kittens you ever saw. They were old enough to leave their mother. I couldn't resist and took a chance on Mom letting me keep one. I picked out the biggest and most aggressive of the bunch and carried him home, praying all the way.

When I walked into the kitchen, Mom threw up her arms and said something like "Lord have mercy, not another cat and kittens under my feet!"

"Mom," I said, "he's a tomcat and won't have kittens."

"Well, OK," Mom said. "But he's *your* responsibility."

"OK," I replied. "I'll clean up the messes and stuff and feed him." So I got to keep him, and I named him Herbie, after Herbert Hoover.

Herbie grew into a giant of a cat and ruled the neighborhood. The people next door got a little Boston bulldog, full grown, and about the second day, Herbie was sauntering across their back yard, and this dog took after him.

Herbie stopped and waited, and when the dog got about 3 feet from Herbie, ol' Herb tore into him. He scratched and chewed the devil out of him until the bleeding dog took off for the house, a-yipping and a-howling.

The neighbors were pretty sore about it, but I told them, "Don't worry. The dog will leave Herbie alone from now on, and Herbie won't start anything."

I knew old Herb, and that's just the way it worked out. Herbie just ignored the dog after that encounter.

After a few years, we moved to another house only two blocks away. But the first house was next to the river bottom, and Herbie liked to hunt there. He wouldn't stay at the new house.

Three times I walked along the river bottom, calling him. He always came to me, and I'd take him home again. The fourth time he didn't come to me, and we never saw him again.

He was pretty old by then. I hope that he just died of old age. We sure missed ol' Herb, the king of the neighborhood! ❖

Trick or Treat

By Ferne Smith Neeb

We all missed our son after he left for college. After a week in the quiet house, Roberta cried with loneliness and asked for a pet cat. She asked friends, but no one had a cat that needed a home. When Berta began to include a cat in her prayers, I called the two veterinarians in our area. But neither had a homeless kitten or cat.

That month, the poem to be memorized in fifth grade was *The Owl and the Pussycat*. When it was Berta's turn to recite, tears ran down her cheeks. She told her classmates how much she wanted a cat. The next day, Larry gave her a note from his mother: "Our old cat had a litter of two. They're weaned now. We'll keep the mother, but you may have one of the kittens."

That same day, Berta met them—a lively brown male and a shy gray female. She brought the shy one home. Larry already had been calling her Smokey, so Berta kept the name.

They got along beautifully. Smokey had six distinct tones in her meows, each with its own meaning. She learned to jump a ribbon, hide in a shoe, and turn the spinner of any board game.

For seven years in Indiana, she was a house cat, content to sit on a windowsill and watch the world go by. When we moved to dairy-farm country in New York state, however, the birds, chipmunks and other small animals in our yard lured her outdoors. We put her on a 40-foot cord fastened to her harness. The rock garden that surrounded a tree just outside the kitchen door was her favorite place. She watched, argued with and stalked every living thing.

She climbed the tree and caught many creatures, even without front claws. She brought her

Roberta and Smokey.

trophies to the back door, jingled her tags with one paw, and then laid the catch at our feet.

One evening, the Ladies Aid group from church was meeting in our living room. I heard Smokey's signal and let her in quickly so I could go back to the meeting. There she laid a mouse, very much alive, at my feet. Eleven women ran in all directions. All Smokey wanted was a word of praise for doing what comes naturally to cats.

On Oct. 30, she spent most of the day in the Indian summer sunshine. She didn't come when we called her for dinner. She wasn't even fastened to her cord. For the first time ever, she was on her own. Tomorrow was Halloween. Was this a prank by neighborhood children to introduce Smokey to the goblins and witches? We called her often during the evening. No Smokey.

A loud meow woke me at 5 a.m. I was so happy to see her that I scooped her up in my arms. *Phew!* I knew that odor, and it was awful! Smokey had had her first battle with a skunk— and the skunk had won.

According to Berta's cat book, the home remedy for skunk odor was a tomato-juice bath. I didn't have any juice, so I put two cans of tomatoes in the blender, made some, and warmed it. I expected a messy bath with an angry cat, so I put on a raincoat and shower cap and took cat and juice to the basement. I scrubbed her with a brush and rinsed her thoroughly. She accepted the unusual bath as if she appreciated it. She even uttered a purr of thanks.

After a rubdown, she looked much better, but she still had a hint of *eau de skunk* about her.

Smokey was our first trick-or-treater that Halloween. She was no treat, but we were thankful to have her home safely. ❖

A Kitten Named Santa Claus

By Dorothy Ward Sylvia

After Papa died, we 8-year-old twins and Mama went to live with Grandpa, Grandma and Aunt Susan so that Mama, now our breadwinner, might work in the shoe factory downtown. Looking back now, over half a century, to that first Christmas without Papa, this is a treasured memory. It began one bleak December day when we children were trudging home from school in a blustery New England snowstorm.

"Only 10 days to Santa Claus!" I shouted.

"Hey, stupid!" our skinny, somber-faced little pal, Rosie Smith, yelled back against the gale. "Don't you know there ain't no Santa Claus? He's just a big lie that rich folks tell their kids to make them be good, else they don't get nothin' for Christmas. Phooey!"

> *"Don't you know there ain't no Santa Claus? He's just a big lie."*

She scuffed her bulky, black, hand-me-down boots through the soft snow, blinked her beady brown eyes and sniffed hard as she wiped her ragged red mittens, first one, then the other, across her drippy little freckled pug nose and glowing cheeks.

"Doesn't Santa Claus come to your house, Rosie?" I asked innocently as we turned into our driveway.

"Of course not!" she snapped, ducking her red tam-o'-shanter against the sharp wind. Then she dashed across our lawn to her home.

That night, when I told Mama about Rosie, she said, "Well, dear, I have to tell you that Rosie is right. Your father was Santa Claus, so now there is no Santa for you twins, either."

Noting the sadness in Mama's eyes, I said cheerfully, "That's all right. We'll be our own Santa Claus, won't we, Sis?"

I glanced hopefully across the room at my stoical twin. We might have looked identical, both being chubby, blued-eyed, blond and freckled, and our voices might have sounded alike, but our thinking definitely was *not* identical. Ethel would quietly study each situation and make up her own mind about it, but I had to learn the art and value of golden silence, slowly and painfully.

"You are brave children," our mother said, "but there is no money to spend for Christmas."

"Not even 10 cents for each gift?" I asked hopefully.

"That depends upon how many are to receive gifts," Mama replied.

I looked pleadingly at Ethel, still sitting cross-legged on the saggy old sofa, sizing up the situation with that familiar "What's she up to now?" look of hers.

"Help me count noses!" I ordered excitedly.

So together we counted on our fingers: Grandpa, Grandma, Mama, Aunt Susan, Uncle Mike, Rosie and us twins.

"That's 80 cents," my twin volunteered.

Mama listened with quiet interest, then announced, "I can give you $1, and you girls will have to decide the best way to use it."

"Oh, goody!" I shouted. "Let's start planning!"

In those days, packing boxes made of wood were plentiful, so the grocer, Mr. Gibson, gladly gave us one about 15 inches deep, with a 16 x 20-inch lid. When we told him it was to be used in place of Santa's pack, he put in some white wrapping paper to line it and a sheet of red and green tissue.

Thereafter, when we twins were missing, we could be found kneeling, squatting, stooping and whispering over that big box on the parlor floor between the two front windows, surrounded by crayons, paste, wrapping paper, scissors and a ball of bright red yarn Grandma had given us. For decorations, we gathered red berries, sweetbrier, pine branches and cones, trailing evergreen and silver-gray bayberries from the nearby woods.

On the lid of the box, I printed "Merry Christmas To All." At first, Ethel objected to this, saying that she did not see how we could be merry without Papa there, and this was understandable because she was his favorite. This bond was established the day we twins were born. Ethel's prospects for survival were very poor, but Papa pointed to his littler twin and said, "Take as good care of her as you do the other one. This one is Papa's boy," a name that stuck to his rugged little pal until after he died.

But when Grandma told us how proud Papa would be to know that his twins were making folks happy on Christ's birthday, Ethel withdrew her objection to the "Merry Christmas" greeting. Quietly, she slipped away and got Papa's picture, which she placed on a small stand overlooking the spot of festivity.

During Christmas week, Aunt Susan took us to the 5-and-10-cent store in Brockton.

Such excitement and long, whispered consultations and decisions, for, incredible as it may seem, one could buy rather nice gifts for 10 cents! There were handkerchiefs, ribbons, pads of paper, pencils, fancy cookie cutters, pretty matchboxes, five 2-cent postage stamps, candy, fruit, vases and many other things from which to make our choices.

Our family was cautioned not to let Rosie know what was under the sheet covering Santa's box. Her mother, Mrs. Smith, had promised that Rosie could come over for breakfast on Christmas morning, and we wanted to surprise her.

All presents were to be left near the box, and we would attach a long string to each package to pull out the gifts.

"Write clearly the name of the person for whom each package is intended," cautioned Aunt Susan.

"Yes, and don't spend over 10 cents on any present, either," Ethel warned, looking directly at me.

Uncle Mike had agreed to come early from Boston where he lived and have breakfast with us. When the 8:15 trolley stopped out front to let him off, Rosie was to come over.

We loved Uncle Mike. He was four years older than Mama and 14 years older than Aunt Susan. However, in spite of his jolly way with us kids, there was a sadness about him, and, if caught off-guard, he looked as if a heavy load bore down on his shoulders, but he didn't want anyone to know how much it hurt. The hurt had come in his eyes and lines in his face after he lost his wife, our lovely Aunt Edna.

We twins must have been a welcome sight to Uncle Mike each Sunday as he alighted from the trolley car and saw us racing to meet him with outstretched arms, telling him to hurry because breakfast (or dinner) was ready and we were hungry. I can see his gaunt, clean-shaven face under his black derby hat as he strode along in shiny-toed black shoes, his long arms swinging and a lively niece skipping along on each side, trying to keep pace.

That early Christmas morning, after we removed the sheet that covered Santa's box, it was a wonderful sight to us twins, equaled

only by the sight of Rosie bouncing in at Uncle Mike's heels.

Rosie looked like a miniature Santa Claus in her long red coat, black boots, fuzzy red tam-o'-shanter and big smile. She must have worked for hours curling strips of white tissue paper to make the clumsy beard. Under one arm she hugged a beautiful wreath her mother had made from pines, evergreens, red berries and white everlasting flowers, topped by a big, red bow of crepe paper.

During the excitement of happy greetings, Grandma rang the breakfast bell. We managed to calm down long enough for Grandpa to ask the blessing at the table, but just as soon as we had eaten our enticing breakfast of hot griddle-cakes, butter, maple syrup and tiny sausages, we gathered around the box. We twins, Aunt Susan and Rosie sat on the floor, and our elders brought their chairs to form a semicircle around us.

Aunt Susan was remarkably young at heart in spite of the heavy responsibilities of this family, and she could be depended upon to aid and abet us in these fun projects. Children were very dear to her. On this special and wonderful Christmas morning, Aunt Susan was like an excited and happy big sister to us. She was our mastermind in our planning and operation. With schoolmarm efficiency, this wise lady suggested that we twins do the pulling of the gifts from the box because we had placed them there and would know best how to retrieve them by the strings. Aunt Susan deciphered the homemade labels, and Rosie was delegated to deliver each gift to the proper recipient.

In an amazingly short and happy time, Santa's box was emptied of gifts and filled with gay, discarded wrappings. When the lid was closed, Uncle Mike put a beautiful box of Christmas candy and sugared popcorn balls on top, calling to everyone to pitch in and enjoy them. When Rosie got up, she placed her mother's pretty wreath with Grandma's gifts with a shy smile.

Suddenly, Ethel remembered something and hopped over to whisper in Aunt Susan's ear. Then, quickly and mysteriously, she disappeared down the cellar steps.

"Attention, everyone!" Aunt Susan commanded. "While Ethel is looking for a little forgotten gift, please pile your presents in front of you so we can all see them and decide which gift merits a prize for being the happiest Christmas gift of all."

It was terribly exciting! Then, right in the midst of this, Ethel returned holding a tiny yellow-and-white kitten. It had a tinkly bell on the red ribbon around its neck, and a card that read, "To Rosie from Santa Claus."

How tenderly that rough little mistress took the mewing, blue-eyed kitten from Ethel's hands!

"Your mother said you could keep it," Ethel assured her.

"All right, everyone!" Aunt Susan called out. "Just whisper your choice of the best fit as I come to you and I will write it down."

When she had gathered all the votes, she burst out laughing. "You'll never believe this, never!" she exclaimed. "Three votes are for the kitten and five votes are for the wreath!"

Everyone clapped and shouted, "The wreath! The wreath! Rosie's mother gets the prize!"

I reached behind the bookcase for a small, package marked "Merry Christmas to the winner" and dropped it into Rosie's lap. I cautioned her not to open it, as it was for her mother.

"I don't have to look," she said triumphantly. "It's just like the package your mother got," she said, pointing.

All eyes turned to Mama's little pile of gifts. Why, of course! It was that small glass ball in which there was a small crèche and two tiny trees. When you shook the glass ball, something like snow settled on the miniature scene so that it looked like the big, snow-covered crèche standing between the two real trees in front of our church uptown.

Rosie jumped to her feet, cuddling the kitten in her neck. "Hold my things while I get dressed," she commanded. "I'm taking Santa Claus home. That's my kitten's name."

We all stood at the window watching her trip across the snowy field, one hand swinging a bag of gifts and goodies, and the other holding a wide-eyed ball of fur with two tiny pointed ears that kept bobbing up over her shoulder.

"Long live Santa Claus," Aunt Susan sighed.

"Amen!" shouted Grandpa.

And we all laughed. ❖

Cat of the Wrong Stripe

By Geraldine Stafford Barton

All of my life, I have had a real fondness for cats, perhaps because there are very few animals as devious as a cat. When I was a child in the early 1900s, we owned a large dairy farm. Dad kept a nondescript old mother cat for a mouser to keep mice out of the feed bins. Each year she had kittens. Homely as they were, I loved this old cat and her kittens. We were not allowed to take them into the house; they had a job to do, and that was to hunt at the barn. Even the cats worked on our farm.

However, I had seen pictures of Persian and Maltese cats, cats of ease and luxury with beautiful bushy tails, not homely old barn cats like ours. My heart yearned for one of these really nice cats.

One beautiful, sunny morning in haying time, my sister, Gladys, and I were sent by my father to the pasture to get the horses. He had hay to put up in the barn. We were not to "dally" around. He was in a hurry, so we scurried up the lane to the pasture in our bare feet.

Along the edge of the lane was our 3-acre field of potatoes, in full bloom. Our eyes nearly popped out when we spied a beautiful, plumy, black-and-white tail, standing straight up, walking up a row in the midst of the potato field. Surely here was my dream come true!

Gladys and I consulted on how to catch our prize. It did not occur to us that the nearest city was 10 miles away and that two smaller towns were in between, and none of our neighbors had any rare cats with bushy tails. We simply decided to sneak through the fence at the end of the field and each take the row on either side of the one he was in. When we got to him, we would grab him.

We tiptoed along in our bare feet. He managed to ignore us completely and kept his nose down, searching the ground. Our presence did not seem to bother him at all. Finally we caught up with him and made a lunge to grab him.

Words cannot describe what happened next. It seemed as if the air for 10 miles was polluted with the most evil smell I had ever smelled. One message did get through to me loud and clear, however: I had picked the wrong cat.

We reacted just about the same as our two shepherd dogs did many years later when they took on a mother skunk and her four babies who were out for a stroll on our lawn. When that skunk got done with them, they were rolling on the ground and pawing at their eyes. When they got up, they yipped around in circles for about 5 minutes.

When we could breathe again, we went on to get the horses. But they didn't want anything to do with us, so they headed for the barn on a dead run.

Our father could smell us long before we arrived. He always "passed the buck" to our mother when it came to punishment; "Go and tell your mother," he said.

We found her down in the garden, weeding onions—but that was not all. My Uncle Claude was standing there, talking with her. *Anyone but him!* He was a real joker. Of course, they smelled us long before we arrived.

Uncle Claude doubled over and laughed till he almost split his sides. His remarks do not bear repeating, but at every family gathering after that, he would snidely remark, "Have you caught any cats lately?"

Mother was furious. She ordered us to get a pail of soap and water on the back porch and scrub and scrub and scrub. We were not go into the house until we did!

Needless to say, this dampened our ardor for strange and rare cats from then on. Thus the moral of the story is "Look before you leap." ❖

That Barn Cat!

By Lorene Sullivan

My husband's parents lived on a farm in the 1940s. Mom was a very timid, shy and unassuming person who appreciated the little things in life. Her eyes would sparkle as she showed you a beautiful flower, a ripe peach or the latest litter of new kittens.

The kittens were always fed at the barn after milking was done. Mom always helped to milk, winter and summer. She watched the kittens grow, but she never attempted to make pets of any of them. They seemed to know the barn was their territory. The house and back porch were off limits—Rover saw to that!

One year, however, something was different. After feeding at the barn, one kitten would follow Mom to the house. Rover let him know he wasn't welcome on the porch, so the cat found a spot near the garden gate where he could watch Mom.

Whenever she left the house to go to the chicken lot, the outhouse, the orchard, the garden or the mailbox, that kitten would follow like a shadow. He never followed anyone else—ever! We all noticed and teased Mom a little about her "shadow."

One summer evening while they were milking their six cows out in the barn lot, the cat came closer and closer to Mom's cow, meowing impatiently for his supper. She was a little aggravated and squirted milk at him, thinking he'd go off and lick himself—but no, that's all it took for him to stand right up on his haunches, ready for the next taste. He got very good at anticipating the stream of milk, and he seldom had to lick much off. Now Mom had a companion at milking time.

Mom never admitted to "loving" this cat, but once in a while, we'd see her stroke his back when he rubbed against her and she thought they were alone.

Can you train a barn cat? Absolutely, I believe, if the cat wants to be trained. Mom's cat proved the point: Lots of attention holds the key; affection just comes naturally. ❖

The author's mother and her cat companion at milking time, August 1941.

Our Sweet Humphrey

By Irma W. Taylor

I love animals. I've had many kinds, but my favorite was a yellow tomcat we called Humphrey. He was born in 1942 in a factory in a Wilmington, Del., suburb where a friend of my husband's worked. Humphrey was skinny and full of fleas. Our friend felt sorry for him, and although he was not supposed to have pets in his apartment, he brought the cat home.

To get rid of the fleas, he sprayed it with outdoor bug spray, then left for the evening. The spray burned the poor kitten's skin. When he licked himself, it burned his tongue and mouth, and it got in his eyes. The poor thing cried so loudly that the landlady heard it. She came up to the apartment and found the kitten. She bathed it as best she could, but when our friend came home, she told him he would have to get rid of it. Knowing that we loved animals, he brought Humphrey to us.

We took him to the vet to be treated. We spent many days thereafter washing his eyes and mouth with the medicine the vet gave us. It was a lot of trouble, but Humphrey proved to be worth it.

Humphrey was the gentlest, sweetest cat I ever had. He let the children dress him in doll clothes. They pushed him around in their baby doll carriage. They put him in a doll high chair, and he ate his meals there.

When he grew older and larger, we bought a child's second-hand high chair for him. He would climb in it and sit there for hours. We gave him birthday parties and invited the neighborhood children. He always entertained them. He even wore a party hat.

Humphrey was an indoor cat, but we put a halter and leash on him and took him for walks. He was so smart. He begged like a dog, jumped through a hoop and would retrieve a large marble.

He grew up with our children and lived to be 18 years old. Yes, Humphrey was special. ❖

Above left: The author's daughter cuddles with Humphrey.
Above right: Humphrey models the latest fashion in doll clothes.
Below: Humphrey ready for dinner and waiting in his favorite chair.

We Called Him Tammy

By John Joseff

The year was 1952, and we lived in Islip, N.Y. Our home was on Tappan Avenue, near a beautiful lake.One day while driving home, my wife, Jeanne, was shocked to see a baby kitten, barely able to walk, on the roadway. She immediately stopped the car. The kitten looked like a newborn, and Jeanne brought it home.Our 9-year-old son, Gary, was thrilled about our newfound friend. We all decided to give the hapless kitten a home. Gary named him Tammy. The name was derived from the lyric of a popular song being sung at that time by Elvis Presley, a great favorite of Gary's.

From that point on, the adventures of Tammy became synonymous with numerous happy and exciting events.

Jeanne tenderly cleaned off the little thing and arranged a basket with a soft cushion. She found a doll's baby bottle somewhere, filled it with warm milk, and Tammy immediately found it to his liking. Jeanne became the mother.

On occasion, Jeanne would sit on the step of our front porch and feed Tammy with the little bottle of milk while two or three neighborhood children looked on in wonderment. It was an exciting moment for all. Tammy was now a permanent member of our family.

As he matured into a full-grown feline, handsome, with gray and white markings, he took over the household, coming and going as he pleased. He was very independent but loving. He and Gary became inseparable at home.

Gary and Tammy.

Tammy would sit midway on the stairs, and when Gary passed by, Tammy would swipe at his head with a paw through the railing. Then down the stairs he'd come, grabbing our son by the pants leg.

In the '50s, young teens wore crewcut hairstyles and used a pomade to keep the hair upright. Our son was in tune with the times, and whenever Gary dozed off on our sofa, Tammy would jump atop the sofa armrest, move into position and lick the top of Gary's crewcut. The pomade had a tantalizing effect on Tammy. It was a sight to see.

From our bedroom we had a beautiful view of a scenic back yard with trees, shrubs and flowers. Beneath our bedroom window, next to a patio deck, I had arranged a pile of cordwood for the fireplace in the winter.

Tammy had the run of the house, sleeping on our bed in the daytime and roaming out-doors at night. Many an early morning, after a night out on the town, he would jump up on the pile of cordwood beneath our bedroom window and scratch on the window screen. He knew Jeanne would get up and let him in for breakfast, a small bowl of milk. Then off he'd go to a cushion somewhere for a snooze.

Tammy also learned how to sit on the edge of the commode seat in our bathroom and relieve himself. This was an amazing feat.

Tammy was no ordinary cat. Some of the things he did were uncanny! One accomplishment in particular always made us wonder in amazement.

In the mid-'50s, we were finally able to enjoy vacation travels all over this magnificent country via the automobile. But who would take care of Tammy?

Jeanne's mother lived about 2 miles north of our home along a busy corridor and across the railroad tracks from the railroad station. She accepted the responsibility. But we learned, to our sorrow and dismay, that Tammy always left her house and found his way back to our home after dark. Then, no doubt fearful at not finding us home, he would walk all the way back to Mother's house. His paws would be sore and red.

But when we returned from our vacation one early evening, there was Tammy, sitting and waiting for our return. We could tell he was one happy cat. We were *all* happy.

Tammy had an ideal sense of direction and belonging coupled with love for us. He belonged only to us, with a deep devotion.

We had Tammy for 12 years before he dragged himself home one night after being run over by a car. Jeanne made him comfortable and took him to a veterinarian.

When we learned Tammy's back was fractured, we knew that permanent sleep was the only answer. We were devastated.

Tammy was more than just a cat. Our memories of him have never left us. Whenever I hear that name, I smile. ❖

Grayola

By Doris Krugen

It was back in the 1930s. I recall living on a farm in southern Minnesota. My parents had six children. We four girls had kittens to play with, and one special one named Grayola. She was gray and very lovable. We dressed her in doll clothes, and she enjoyed many rides in the doll carriage. She always gave us a "jump" when we picked her up.

In 1938, my parents moved 4 miles away, and Grayola went with us. Some time later, however, she came up missing.

Many months passed. Then, one day, a tired kitten came by. She was very skinny and run-down. We girls picked her up, and there was that little "jump." "That's Grayola!" we all said. We figured she must have gone back to the first farm and then returned to us.

I am now 82 years young and living in an apartment in east central Minnesota. As I recall these memories from the Good Old Days, it seems like only yesterday. ❖

1929 *The Farmer's Wife*, House of White Birches nostalgia archives

Tiger

By Darryl E. Matter
with Roxana Marie Matter

*I*t was in the summer of 1933 when my cousin, Frank, and I built our catapult. I had studied about this ancient weapon in the eighth grade and wanted to see if I could build one. (The thought of being able to use it to hurl rocks through the air excited me.)

Frank, who was two years older than I and lived with us on our farm, was an inventive genius who was good at making things out of scraps. (He, too, looked forward to having a catapult and had some ideas of his own.)

Together we constructed our catapult. Lumber came from our scrap pile, and Frank salvaged a large spring from a worn-out farm implement for motive power. It took a great deal of energy to compress the spring, so we believed—correctly, we later determined—that our catapult would be exceedingly powerful. We found that it was capable of throwing a moderately heavy rock almost 100 yards, the length of a football field.

For several days, Frank and I amused ourselves by hurling rocks over the garage and into the pond on the other side. Then Frank brought out some firecrackers. We tied a large firecracker to a rock and lit the fuse just before releasing the catapult. The rock and firecracker went high into the air. *BANG!* The firecracker exploded way up in the air.

Most of the family thought it was fun to see the firecrackers explode high overhead. Even Bossy, the family milk cow, seemed to think it was fun. She didn't pay any attention to the noise. Instead, she seemed to watch Frank and me out of the corner of her eye.

One day while I was eating breakfast, I happened to notice old Tiger, Mom's aged yellow cat. He usually sat or slept peacefully on a window ledge where he could soak up the sunshine and watch what was going on outside. Tiger was so tame that he'd let anyone pick him up—a fatal flaw!

I explained my plan to Frank, and he agreed to help. We found a small basket that Tiger sometimes slept in and fastened it to our catapult. After we cocked the catapult, I kidnapped Tiger and carried him to the machine. Then we placed him in the basket. After a few moments of petting, Tiger went right to sleep.

"OK," whispered Frank, "he's asleep."

I pulled the rope to release the catapult.

Tiger was so tame that he'd let anyone pick him up—a fatal flaw!

There was a *whoosh!* as the spring propelled the catapult arm into motion and then a loud *clunk!* as it reached its stopping point.

"What are you boys doing?" Mom called from the kitchen window—just as I pulled the rope. Mom came out of the house just in time to see Tiger go flying through the air. (She later insisted that his legs were outstretched stiff, his tail was rigid, and his hair was on end!) I could see that his mouth was open, but there was no sound coming from him. Up over the garage he went!

Mom, Frank and I ran around the garage to see what was happening. We heard a loud *ker-splash!* as Tiger landed in the pond. Soon he surfaced and swam for the shore. Mom didn't find much humor in the incident.

As for Tiger, he didn't seem much the worse for the experience. He continued his frequent naps in the window, but I noticed that he followed Mom wherever she went and kept an eye on Frank and me whenever we were around. One thing I'll bet: Old Tiger never forgot that trip he took in our catapult. ❖

A Catastrophe

Three gay little kittens, named Black,
White and Gray,
From their own cozy corner
once wandered away.
And old Mother Catkins, asleep
on her chair,
Ne'er dreamed that her babies
were "off on a tear."

The kitty-cats frolicked,
and gambolled, and ran,
And cut up such capers as only cats can;
And when they encountered
a very high wall,
Up scrambled and clambered
the little cats all.

"We're out for a high-time,"
the kitty-cats said;
And they danced a few quick-steps;
turned heels over head;
Then Whitey and Graycoat
struck up a sweet tune,
While Black sat sedately
and mewed at the moon.

But brief was their pleasure.
They soon heard a yell
Of "Scat there, you cats there!"
while shoes and things fell.
Down scrambled and tumbled
the poor little kits,
And scampered off homeward,
scared out of their wits.

With joy, their warm corner
the runaways spied;
And when they were nestled
by old Catkins' side,
The kittens purred softly,
"No more will we roam,
For all the world over,
there's no place like home."

—E. Louise Liddell

Two Kittens

Two little kittens, one stormy night,
Began to quarrel and then to fight.
One had a mouse,
the other had none,
And that was the way
the quarrel begun.

"I'll have that mouse,"
said the bigger cat.
"You'll have that mouse!
We'll see about that!"
"I will have that mouse,"
said the elder son.
"You shan't have that mouse!"
said the little one.

I told you before
'twas a stormy night
When these two kittens
began to fight;
The old woman seized
her sweeping-broom,
And swept the two kittens
right out of the room.

The ground was covered
with frost and snow,
And the two little kittens
had nowhere to go;
So they laid them down
on the mat at the door
While the old woman finished
sweeping the floor.

Then they crept in
as quiet as mice,
All wet with snow
and as cold as ice,
For they found it was better,
that stormy night,
To lie down and sleep
than to quarrel and fight.

—Author unknown

Jim Daly
©
1991

One in a Million

By Aline Soukup

*D*iamonds might be most girls' best friend, but not mine. One of my best friends, a stray cat, brought me greater pleasure than any diamond could. This lovable cat came into my life at the right time and place, and she was responsible for a chain of events so unusual that they evolved into an unforgettable story and memory.

World War II had great bearing on this cat tale, for I'd have never owned a cat if my husband, Jim, had not been stationed at an Air Force base in Texas during the war.

As newlyweds, we hated being separated during the first six months of his service, so when he came home to Pittsburgh on his first furlough and suggested I go back to Texas with him, I jumped at the chance.

I quit my job and joined thousands of other Army wives who followed their husbands from camp to camp, hoping the war would end before their loved ones were shipped overseas.

How could a Texas cat know about Pennsylvania coal dirt and snow?

The place we called home in Texas was a little cabin in a tourist court. All the rental housing in the small town was taken, and waiting lists were long, so the cabin at the tourist court was the next best thing. The homesickness that prevailed among the servicemen and their wives rubbed off on me. Jim showered me with empathy, for he had just survived six months of coping with the homesick blues, and he knew exactly how I felt.

During the week after Jim returned to the base, he noticed a cat loafing around the hangars. As each day went by, the stray reminded Jim more and more of me, so by the end of the week, after checking to make sure no one at the field owned the cat, he brought her home to me. To say I was surprised is putting it mildly; shocked is more like it.

This was a rare move—actually a sacrifice on Jim's part. He was a hunter and a friend of animals, but he didn't exactly like cats. Yet he was prepared to do anything to chase away my blues. Besides, there was a method to his madness: The cat would get rid of the pesky mice around the tourist court.

I welcomed the cat with wide-open arms and heart, and since her snow-white fur was blotched with patches of brown and black, I appropriately named her Calico. She seemed to sense that she was meant to be my companion, and she seldom strayed from the courtyard.

Calico not only kept me company, but she entertained me. She was adept at catching mice, and every so often, she brought a live one into the cabin, both to show me she was doing her job and to entertain me.

Calico and the mouse usually performed under the kitchen table. Holding the captured mouse gently in her paws, Calico would suddenly release the mouse, allow it to go so far, then, quicker than a flash, reach out one paw and recapture it. This was repeated over and over.

Only once did the mouse escape into an opening in the floor. Calico was mortified! She crouched beside that hole for the rest of the day, waiting for the mouse to return.

Of course, it never did.

It seemed to me that Calico was deliriously happy to have a place to call home, and she had no intentions of straying. There was no need for her to stray, for the neighborhood cats visited her daily. By the time Jim's next furlough rolled around, the three of us were so bonded that there was no question about taking Calico home to Pittsburgh with us, despite the long, tedious ride that we knew might be troublesome.

The servicemen who lived in town sought rides to and from the base with soldiers who had cars, and since Jim had brought me back to Texas in our car, it was packed with riders daily. One passenger who was scheduled for furlough the same time as Jim made arrangements for him and his wife to travel as far as Indiana with us. An unmarried buddy also made plans to accompany us all the way to Pittsburgh.

When we picked up the Indiana couple, the wife stepped into the car carrying a small box punctured with holes, and when she saw Calico, she cried out, "Oh, no!"

When the rest of us realized she had a canary in the box, we echoed her sentiments. This weird situation instantly set the tone of the trip.

None of us will ever forget that journey. Whenever the canary fluttered or chirped, Calico

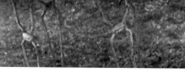

Calico made herself to home.

went berserk, leaping over all of us, shedding fur along the way. When the bird was quiet, Calico rested on the back-window ledge, staring at the box, ready to pounce the instant the bird made a sound.

We sighed with relief when the frustrated couple and the frightened bird finally departed in Indiana. A subdued Calico purred contentedly and seemed to enjoy the rest of the ride, but we spent the rest of the trip attempting to remove the cat hairs that were glued to our clothes.

When we arrived at my parents' home, they couldn't believe Calico had traveled from Texas in the car with *us*, let alone with a canary. They welcomed Calico, but she was disoriented and sought a place to hide. She discovered an open door to the basement and disappeared for a long while. When she reappeared we were astonished to see an all-black cat! She had discovered the coal bin.

Calico was very, very busy licking coal dust from her fur for the extent of our stay. She balked at venturing outdoors in the snowy, cold weather, so she visited the coal bin often.

Poor thing! How could a Texas cat know about Pennsylvania coal dirt, snow and freezing temperatures? But class act that she was, Calico adjusted quite well. When we left my parents' house, her white fur was more beautiful than ever from the daily lickings.

In Texas, where the weather was mild most of the time, the door to our cabin was always left ajar so Calico could come and go without disturbing us—*except one night*. Calico awakened me with loud meowing as she sat like a statue in front of the cardboard clothes cupboard.

Ignoring my whispered pleas for quiet, she only meowed louder and refused to budge from her position in front of the cupboard.

On impulse, I turned on the light and raised the cupboard door. Calico immediately leaped into the cupboard and began to purr quietly in a welcome contrast to her insistent meows.

Although peace and quiet were restored, something urged me to find a flashlight and investigate. Then I discovered an adorable kitten in my shoe! She was a carbon copy of Calico, right down to the brown and black patches. What a surprise! We had never suspected Calico was pregnant; she had never grown fat or appeared to be carrying a litter.

Question after question tormented us, and none was answered. We wondered how Calico and her newborn had ended up in the cupboard when its door was always kept closed. Evidently it had been left open once, and Calico was in the right place at the right time. Several cat owners advised us that cats never have a litter of only one, and we entertained the thought that Calico might have had a larger litter outside the cabin. Perhaps the kitten in my shoe was the lone survivor. We considered the possibility that Calico could have stolen the kitten, but I had a problem believing that. Calico was the only calico cat in a neighborhood full of ordinary gray cats. That combination couldn't create a calico cat, could it?

We weren't granted time to dwell on these questions. We soon realized that the kitten wasn't thriving; it looked frail and weak. We examined Calico only to find she didn't have any milk. The tiny newborn hadn't been receiving any milk from her and was probably dying. We tried to feed the kitten milk with an eyedropper, but it didn't work. The little bundle of fur died. The mystery of its birth was buried with it. Calico was listless after the death of the kitten, and this may have contributed to her own death under a speeding car on the highway at the entrance of the tourist court.

Though Calico's life with us was short, she packed that time with unforgettable memories. When I browse through my albums and come across pictures of Calico, a warm glow surrounds me, reminding me of the best animal friend I ever had. ❖

My Tiger

By Harold Eslie Gordon

I grew up in Maine, and, as a 6-year-old, I wanted a dog. But Dad said, "No, I have enough mouths to feed." I asked my dad if I could have a cat. He said, "No, we don't need a cat either."

Well, things were real hard back in those days in the early 1930s. I started school in a two-room schoolhouse with no plumbing. We took turns carrying our water from a spring in the woods. We walked to school back in those days.

As I was walking home from school with my best friend one day, he told me they had four kittens to give away. I said, "My dad won't let me have a cat."

But my friend's dad said, "Take one home. If he won't let you keep it, you can bring it back." The kitten was 8 weeks old. I took it home in a cracker box and placed it on the table where Dad was reading.

"What have you got there?" he asked. He opened the box. In it was a tiger kitten with a bobtail. Dad fell in love with it.

"Can I keep it?" I asked.

"I guess so," he answered. Whenever my dad said "I guess so," he meant "yes."

Dad taught Tiger to do tricks. He showed all our visitors how his cat could roll over on command. He was really proud of that cat.

When I got older, our neighbor got a big, black dog. They named him Joe Louis. Their boy didn't care about the dog, so I played with him a lot. Joe Louis would go down to the stream with me. He loved the water. He taught me to dog-paddle, and soon I was a good swimmer too.

After I left home, old Tiger stayed with my dad. He was his pride and joy. Now, here I am, almost 76 years old, and I feel Dad and old Tiger are up above, watching over me. ❖

A Cat to Remember

By Doris C. Crandall

*I*n the Dust Bowl days of the 1930s, many of our neighbors gave up trying to make a living from the topsoil-less land in the Texas Panhandle. Just like the families in John Steinbeck's book *The Grapes of Wrath*, they loaded meager belongings into old cars and trucks and headed for California. Our friends couldn't take everything they owned with them, and one family left their white Persian cat with us.

We really didn't need a cat. Not that kind of cat, anyway. We already had seven regular, hardworking, no-favors-asked farm cats. "That cat won't fit in," I said to Mama.

"Shush," she replied. "We're lucky. The Everest family left their *grandpa* with the Petersons. 'Too old to make the journey,' they said."

Well, I thought, *better a cat than a grandpa. At least the cat can stay outside.*

Wrong! The new cat prissed into our house on her little furry feet, pranced around in front of everybody and showed off fit to strangle. She looked at me with her one blue eye and one green eye and said "Meow" in the softest cat voice I'd ever heard. But she didn't melt my hard-hearted resolve. I put her outside. We had never allowed our farm cats inside the house, and Queenie would just have to cope the best way she could.

I changed her name to Mrs. Cunning. Queenie sounded like royalty, and we didn't tolerate supremacy. We treated each cat the same and each had to catch its own share of mice.

Mrs. Cunning didn't like to catch mice. She preferred to lounge on a pillow and have meals brought in. Would she line up with the other cats and catch the milk Daddy squirted straight from the cows as he milked? Never! She insisted on having her milk in a saucer, and she drank with one dainty paw steadying the bowl. She reminded us of a society lady drinking tea with her pinkie stuck out.

Her uppity ways riled us so much we began to call her "that cat." She even irked the farm cats, and they wouldn't so much as meow at her.

That cat sneaked into the house every chance she got. We locked her out at night, but she outsmarted us on that issue, too. She climbed on top of the house, scratched a hole in the window screen, and came in through an open upstairs window.

I nearly had a "catniption" fit the night she awakened me purring around my face. She had another cute trick up her ruff, too. When she thought she wasn't getting the attention due, she sprang it on me.

Once I was hanging freshly washed clothes on the line in rhythm to my humming *When the Roll Is Called Up Yonder*. Mrs. Cunning was the farthest thing from my mind. She slinked up behind me, sprang onto my back and dug in. I thought I'd been struck by a chicken hawk. I screamed and dropped Daddy's long johns in the dirt.

Then one day, a shorthaired, bluish gray tomcat, handsome in the Rhett Butler style, showed up at our farm. The gay, devilish fellow ignored the young farm females and went after Mrs. Cunning. He got her, and then the scoundrel ran off. We never saw him again.

We couldn't blame Mrs. Cunning; she'd led a sheltered life and probably didn't know any better. Maybe she had fallen in love. We pitied her. She had to raise her litter of shorthaired, multicolored kittens all alone.

After that, Mrs. Cunning gave up her foolish, high-hat ways and began to act like we thought a farm cat should. She learned to catch mice with the best of the cats. She seldom tried to get into the house, and she never again sprang onto my back.

Over the years, all the other cats we reared on our farm blended into one big blur in my mind. But Queenie? Now *there* was a cat to remember. ❖

A Furry Merry Christmas

By Phil Gollihue

I don't quite remember the exact year, but I recall it was very warm for late December. My dad had gone to Michigan to paint houses for my Uncle Bus so we could have a good Christmas. He wasn't due home for another week, and I was missing him something awful.

Back when I was a young'un in West Virginia, it was nothing to find a burlap sack floating down the creek from someplace in Holden or Cora—the coal camps above where I lived—with puppies or kittens tied up in it. That was how folks back then disposed of them in hopes they would drown.

Five little orphans depended on him, and time was running out.

My mom and granny had been taking photos earlier that day to send to my dad to show him how strange the weather was at home. Mom and I were sitting on the creek bank watching the cars on the road across the creek when I spotted the bag as it came floating by. I noticed that the bag was wiggling back and forth in the water.

"Mom, there's something alive in that bag yonder. Can I go fetch it and see what's in it?"

"Now, Phil, you know what your dad told you before he left home. You're not to get into any trouble of any sorts."

I felt a sadness as I watched the sack pass by, for I knew that there were some poor little animals that would die soon without help. Mom, seeing the look on my

© *Favorite Gift* by Jim Daly

face, finally gave in and told me to fetch the sack. I headed down the bank and into the ice-cold water. I didn't waste any time getting out and back up the bank.

"Mom, it's baby kittens. I can hear them."

Mom seemed to be as excited as I was, and she helped untie the sack. We dumped out six small kittens. Five were still alive. They were all tigers, light yellow with stripes.

"Well, son, you've got a job ahead of you. You have to get rid of them before your dad gets home next week."

"But Mom, they're so little they would die if I let 'em go alone without their mommy."

"I'm sorry, son, but you know how your dad feels about cats around his rabbits and guinea pigs. Them cats will eat every one we have, and you know it."

"But what can I do? I just can't let them starve to death."

"That's your worry. Now that you took them from the creek, you figure it out."

For the rest of the afternoon, I played with the homeless babies. I wasn't thinking of what I would do with them. For the next two days, I lost the thought of getting rid of them.

I finally put them in a paper box and went around the camp, trying to find them a home, but to no avail.

After two more days of walking, I still had five orphans. That night, I lay in bed worrying. Then it came to me: It was close to Christmas, and they'd make nice presents for someone.

During the night, the camp had been blanketed by pure white and it was still snowing. Without stopping to eat breakfast, I went flying right on by the table and out the door.

After getting five small boxes from old Tokyo Joe's store, I put a kitten in each one with a little milk, placed them on my home-made sled, and off I went.

About a half mile down from our camp was a small camp we called Tarpaper City. It housed kids less fortunate than we were. It wasn't hard to get rid of the kittens there. All I had to do was make believe I worked for Santa. I told the first one that Santa was really

It was close to Christmas, and they'd make nice presents for someone.

busy and had asked if I would hand out these special gifts. With this small white lie, it didn't take long to find all the kittens a home.

But as you know, a lie will follow a lie; and if you let it go at that, it will soon haunt you, so I told Mom what I had done. She sat me down at the kitchen table.

"Son, you think you did a fine thing by finding them homes, but did you think about Santa? He knows everything you do, and do you think he might just pass you by at Christmas for using his name to trick the kids?"

This hit home. It got me thinking, *It ain't too late; I'll go tell the kids the truth.* I did. But you know, there wasn't *one* of them who would give up his gift from Santa.

So I felt I'd done the right thing. And Santa must have forgiven me, for on Christmas morn, I found under my tree a scooter, some new bibs and brogans. And one more thing—there was a card from Santa himself. It read, "Phil, I want to thank you for helping with my deliveries this year. Signed: Santa Claus." ❖

Boots and Babette

By Juanita Bain

When I was growing up in a small town in Texas, I had a Boston terrier. I named him Boots because he had white on all his legs.

I took piano lessons, and when I practiced, no matter where Boots was, he ran to a chair by the piano, lay down and listened to me.

Now I'm grown and have a cat named Babette. When I play the piano, she runs as far away from me as she can.

What's the difference—my playing, or the animals? ❖

The Three-Colored Cat

By Romaine Mann

The year was 1913, and March was very wet. The little tributaries were bank-full and running into Swatara Creek. The old dam could not hold it all, so the creek went berserk. All of Londonderry Township was flooded. Coming home from market that Saturday morning, the water was 3 feet deep along the road. Our horse, Harry, did not want to get in all that water, but Mom had work to do at home. We had a mile of this deep water. Finally we came to the turn in the road. We saw Nan Shaffer over close to the iron mine bridge. She had her dress twisted up around her waist and was trying to pull something like a chicken-house door out of the bushes.

She finally got it loose and pushed it over to the approach to the bridge. Two chickens flew on the bridge in safety, but Nan still had something in her hand. She tried to talk to us, but the sound of the water at the dam was too great.

When we got home, I asked Mom if she would call Nan. We thought she had been holding a turtle. But Nan told my mother that it was a three-colored kitten about 10 weeks old, and that the kitten's back leg was hurt a little. She washed the mud off the kitten, gave it warm milk and put it under the stove. The kitten must have gone to sleep then.

My mother told us a three-colored cat is supposed to be lucky, but Nan said that Andy (her husband) would not believe old wives' tales.

About nine weeks later, Andy's broker called. He had sold a lot for Andy that they had been trying to sell for six years. Old Andy said, "By gum, that cat sold my lot!"

The three-colored cat grew up, and every time Andy opened the front door, the cat came back and sat on Andy's old wicker chair by the open oven door.

She would jump onto his knees and purr and purr. Old Andy would say, "Pipe down, Patches, I can't hear myself read." But Patches just kept purring.

Nan would stand at the kitchen sink with the dishcloth in her hand and smile to herself. *He loves that cat*, she thought.

One night, Patches did not come home. They called and called, but no cat. Next morning, they started calling again.

A neighbor who joined in the search came out of an old boathouse and said, "Is that your cat? Come here, Andy." Patches had three three-colored kittens in the seat of a big, plush boat.

Andy took the kittens in his arms and carried them home. He put the kittens in a basket behind the stove. Patches took one by the neck and took it over to Andy's chair. Andy said, "No you don't. One cat sitting in my chair is quite enough!" ❖

1956 *Junior Instructor*, courtesy of Janice Tate

On the Wild Side

Chapter Four

When it came to playmates, the best way to find an animal pal was to take a walk on the wild side back in the Good Old Days. I could count the number of domesticated pets—cats, dogs and the like—I had when I was a youngster. But the number of temporary pets I found along the woodland trails near my house probably numbered in the hundreds.

Turtles, rabbits, lizards, frogs and snakes were just a few of the various companions that found their way into my pockets during summer vacations from school. They were always temporary because their friendship only lasted until their discovery by my all-seeing mother.

Probably my greatest fascination with those wild ones began on a walk with my father. I was about 6 years old and we were following a narrow pathway that led to a deep hollow. It was early autumn and the walnut trees had already dropped their leaves, but the oaks and hickories still clung to their cloaks of yellow and red.

Daddy wasn't hunting, but he shushed me anyway—probably just on principle. I was inquisitive about nearly everything I saw, while Daddy was wanting a simple, quiet Sunday afternoon walk.

"God gave you two ears and two eyes, but only one mouth," Daddy said. "He did that so you would listen and see twice as much as you talk." So I locked my lips and kept my ears and eyes tuned to the wonders assaulting my senses on every side.

They plowed through the leaves in a leaping frenzy.

We followed the trail along the ridge to a point overlooking the hollow. For a moment the afternoon was as quiet as Daddy wanted it. The breeze died to a whisper. The cornflake leaves didn't snap, crackle or pop. The scene was as serene as a pew an hour before church. And I couldn't stand it!

"Daddy …?" my question began.

Suddenly the valley exploded into motion. More than a dozen deer had chosen the hollow for a resting place and had frozen in camouflage during our approach. My single, emphatic, shrill word had gouged them into a panic and they plowed through the leaves in a leaping frenzy.

"What's that, Daddy?"

"A herd of deer," he explained as the din was muffled in the distance.

"I want one!" I exclaimed.

I could see no difference between collecting a deer as a pet and the baby bunny I had brought home the previous summer. Both were furry, had a white tail and could really, *really* jump.

Daddy explained that not all of God's creatures were designed for me to tame and introduce to the family. So, of all the animal friends I discovered along the trails of my young life, I never got to call a deer a pet.

The stories in this chapter will reiterate that friendship, like beauty, is in the eyes of the beholder. Sure, a lot of our favorite pets from the Good Old Days came in canine and feline packages. But for a lot of us, our most interesting pals came from a walk on the wild side.

—*Ken Tate*

Facing page: *Rustic Retreat—Whitetail Deer* by Rosemary Millette, courtesy of Wild Wings Inc.

Oscar, Is That You?

By Mary Helen Pelton

This story was told to me by my husband, Ray Pelton. Ray and his family lived on a dairy farm about 8 miles northeast of Dickinson, N.D. During the time of this story, in the early 1950s, Ray and his siblings walked to a one-room school about 2 miles from the family farm.

"O scar, is that you?" gasped Ray as the half-grown buck walked toward him. The buck stopped within a foot of Ray. As Ray reached out to touch the sprouting horns on the animal, the deer raised his head as if in salute and leaped away. As he stared in wonder at the form disappearing over the butte, Ray remembered the first time he had touched Oscar.

Illmar, the hired man, had rushed into the kitchen with tears forming rivulets down his dust-covered checks. He carried something tiny in his massive hands. "He's hurt, Ray. Get your mom. Poor little thing was hiding in the tall grass. Must have just been born. I mowed over him and he squealed like a cat on fire."

Dad came in from the living room. "Hold him, Ray," he commanded. "I'll get the car, and we'll take him to the veterinarian."

"Little fellow weighs about 7 pounds, about the same as a baby."

The tiny speckled fawn shivered in Ray's arms and stared with panicked eyes as Dad raced into town. One of the fawn's legs rested in an unnatural angle.

When they arrived at the office, Doc told them that Illmar got the mower stopped just in time. The only injury he had was the broken leg. They watched as Doc fashioned a tiny splint that held the leg stiff but still allowed the fawn to walk.

"You'll have to feed him, though," Doc said. "His mother will be too frightened by all the man smells to take him back. The fawn should be good in about six weeks, but you might notice a bump on his leg where the break has healed."

When Ray and Dad drove up to their farmhouse, they were met by five anxious faces staring out the window. The younger brothers and sisters tumbled out the door to welcome their newest baby home.

"Let's call him Oscar," said Ginger, the youngest sister. She'd been trying to name everything Oscar—from the youngest brother to the barn cat—with no luck, but this time it stuck. Oscar he became.

Mom had an old pillow ready for Oscar's bed. Each child took a turn petting, feeding and comforting their baby. Gone was Oscar's fear. You could almost see him sigh with contentment. That is, until the chocolate-colored cocker spaniel bounced into the room. Oscar trembled as

Pal took a step forward. Pal tilted his head back and forth as if trying to understand what manner of creature this was. After staring for a tense two minutes, Pal crept forward, licked Oscar's face, then cuddled up on the floor beside him.

Oscar and Pal became fast friends; however, it seemed clear that Oscar thought he was a dog. Oscar and Pal followed Ray as he fed the chickens. They frolicked with the children as they played. They walked with the children the 2 miles to the country school and then chased each other home. Pal and Oscar roamed, chased, charged, dodged, spun and rolled day after day.

One day when Oscar was about six months old, Ray heard laughing and splashing from the bathroom. He ran toward the bathroom door to see water running out from under it. Inside, he found the two youngest kids and Oscar in the bathtub, covered with bubbles. Mother's favorite bubble bath lay empty on the floor.

"Mom's going to kill you when she gets home!" Ray yelled. "Get some rags and clean up this mess! Take Oscar outside—*now*."

Not only was Oscar getting too big for the house, he was getting too big, period. He tried to play with the 4-year-old brother but knocked him to the ground instead. He'd rear back on his hind legs like a stallion and his knife-sharp hooves would slice the air like the sword of a mounted knight. That was the way he and Pal had always played, but one day he cut a 2-inch gash in Pal's shoulder.

"Something has to be done," Mom said. "Had that been one of the children, the child might have been killed. No sense trying to turn him loose; he's always been free to return to the wild. He thinks he belongs here."

After Mom and Dad made three calls, five children and Mother piled into the car. Dad and Ray drove in a pickup with Oscar in the back. They pulled up to a wild animal park about 45 miles from the farm. The children sobbed as Father handed Oscar over to the park's owner.

"You just come back to visit Oscar anytime," he said. "The ticket will be on me."

Four months later, the park owner called. "Gosh, I'm sorry. Oscar jumped the fence, and we can't find him anywhere. Maybe he'll wander back in a while. He doesn't have the wild sense to make it on his own. I'll keep you posted." But he never called again.

Spring came, then summer. The fall air was crisp with the smell of ripening apples. Ray walked past fields of grain dipped low with their heavy heads. Something caught his eye on the distant horizon. An animal was moving toward him across the fields from a large butte.

"Oscar, is that you?" The young buck walked to Ray, searching his face as if for lost memories. As Ray reached out to touch the budding antlers, he noticed the bump on the animal's right leg. As the buck jerked back and turned to run up the butte, Ray whispered, "Looks like he learned to live wild after all." ❖

House of White Birches nostalgic archives

Ken and Captain Flap

By Jane Eisele

We were living in Stillwater, Okla. My son Ken was 11 years old. While walking home from school one day, he saw a baby bird chirping and struggling on the ground. It had fallen from its nest. Ken picked it up and brought it home.

One of its legs was broken, so we got a Popsicle stick, broke it in half and used it for a splint, setting it as best we could, and securing the stick with adhesive tape.

Ken kept him in a box in the garage. He finger-fed the bird soft canned dog food, and the bird seemed to thrive on it. He was getting bigger and stronger. He began wobbling around the garage floor, dragging that bad leg. Then he would eat by himself out of the dog dish, even with our dog.

Now he was getting pretty feathers, so we knew he was a male. He seemed to like all of the family, as any of us could hold him, but he always rode around on Ken's head or shoulder. His home was in the garage, but we left the door open all the time so he could go in and out. He had learned to fly by this time, so Ken had named him Captain Flap. He would come when we called him by name.

One day I was holding him and noticed the splint on the leg was awful tight. I couldn't get it off, so I called a vet. I asked if he treated birds and he said yes. (I didn't tell him we had a blue jay.) We all got in the station wagon. Captain rode on the back of the front seat between Ken and me. When we got out, he jumped onto Ken's shoulder while we walked into the vet's office.

The vet was amazed that he could take the bird from Ken's shoulder and treat him. He removed the splint and said we had done a great job of fixing the leg. I asked what we owed him, and he said not a thing—he was just shocked and amazed to see how Ken had tamed him.

Captain was free to fly wherever, but he knew where home was. Sometimes he would squawk loudly at the door, so we would open the door to the house. He was welcome inside too. He would sit around on the furniture.

We were getting ready to move to Tennessee, so the movers came. Captain was confused as he sat on the couch while the movers put it in the truck; then he flew back in to sit on a chair while they packed it. The movers said they had never packed a truck like that before.

> *Captain would squawk at the door to the house so we would open it.*

We all got in the station wagon. For this long trip, we put Captain in a cage on the backseat. We stopped in St. Louis to see Grandma. Captain was glad to get out of his cage, and he spent most of the time in Grandma's peach tree. But he followed us into Grandma's house too. Then it was back in the car to Tennessee. Captain helped the movers again as they put things into the new house. He liked his new home; he lived in a new garage, but shared our home. He sure amazed our new neighbors. We had him for nearly a year.

One weekend we were planning a camping trip at the lake and were staying in a cabin. Captain was in the tree above the cabin. Ken, his brother Bill, and Dad got in the boat to go fishing. Suddenly a storm came up—rain, wind and lightning. I guess it scared Captain, and he flew off.

When the guys came back, we all called and called for Captain and looked all over, but we couldn't find him. We stayed a few more days, but he never returned. Our family was heartbroken when we had to leave camp without Captain Flap.

Today, Ken is almost 60. But we still think of Captain. ❖

Our Raccoons

By Rev. Carroll A. Ochsner

In 1950, my brother Cecil and I operated a large farm. We had a lot of cattle. We attended a farm auction in the early spring. One of the sale items read, "Barn full of alfalfa hay." We estimated it contained bout 10 tons of hay. We purchased it. About a week later, my brother took the truck and went after the first load. It was a Saturday morning, so he took our children, Juanita and Robert, with him.

When they returned, each child held a raccoon that was just a few days old. They had found the baby raccoons in a couple of bales deep in the hay. I was not too happy, but since they seemed already attached to the animals, I relented and let them keep them.

We rigged up doll bottles with nipples, filled them with cow's milk, and the 'coons ate readily. But those animals cried, mostly at night, for more than two weeks—not so much because they were hungry, but because they missed the warmth of their mother.

Robert feeds one of the raccoons he and Juanita found.

But after about three weeks, they quit crying. In fact, they would jump out of the box and chase each other around the kitchen floor. By this time, they were eating homemade bread and milk. I built them a cage on the south end of our summer kitchen. It had a dark place where they could sleep in the straw.

The 'coons were females. They had no names because we couldn't tell them apart. They were just "the 'coons."

They continued to thrive on bread and milk. I tried them on fresh fish, but they wanted no part of it. When we opened the cage door each morning, they made a dash for the children who were holding their bread and milk.

My uncle owned a grocery store and kept us well supplied with samples of breakfast cereal. One day the kids opened the side of a box for each 'coon, and they ate every morsel. After that, the kids would each hold a box and each animal would take one, put it on the sidewalk, tear it open with sharp claws and eat the contents.

We had a small tractor and a two-wheeled trailer that we used to repair fence on our hilly farm. My brother would drive the tractor and I would lie on my back in the trailer. One 'coon would stand on its hind legs on my forehead, its front legs on the front of the trailer, and the other 'coon would stand on its hind legs on my chest, its claws on the side of the trailer. They would play while we repaired fence. When we were ready to go home, we would give a few whistles, and the 'coons would come running for the ride home.

One night the animals somehow got the cage door open. In the morning, we discovered that they were gone. The kids were devastated, but I tried to cheer them up, as I was pretty sure they would return.

When the kids came home from school, their first question was, "Have you seen the 'coons?" I hadn't, but shortly after dark, Robert heard a scratching on the door. He opened it and the 'coons dashed in, looking for their bread and milk.

They made wonderful pets for the kids for more than two years. They finally died just a couple of days apart. ❖

Robert and Juanita hold the raccoons soon after they found them.

Zeb

By Jay T. Cloud

When I was a boy, farm kids went barefoot in the summertime. At first, when we pulled our shoes off, the soles of our feet were tender. This raised going barefoot to a sort of art form. Walking through wheat stubble, we learned to use sliding steps to bend the stubble and keep it from pricking our feet. A wary eye looked for dewberry vines, which were really briars filled with thorns. Also, we kept a weather eye out for bees and yellow jackets. Naturally, we looked down a lot.

While taking a cool drink to my father who was plowing, I spotted a tiny ball of fur that turned out to be a raccoon.

There was no way of knowing how he got there. My errand completed, I took the baby animal home and put it in a shoebox lined with leaves and wood shavings.

We fed him milk, first with an eyedropper, then with a rubber glove with the small finger punctured. The raccoon recovered and soon graduated to more natural food.

We started him with eggs and small pieces of tuna and salmon. Being omnivorous, he was soon catching insects, eating earthworms and testing plants of his choice.

He proved his ability to forage for himself when he started raiding the garbage pail. Nothing was free from his prying. The sugar bowl, cookie jar, coffee can and utensil drawer all became targets.

The shoebox was no longer adequate, so we moved him to larger quarters on the back porch. At this point, he was bigger and more active, and he pried into everything.

We named him Zeb.

A shepherd puppy my sister named Brutus was his playmate. Their comical rollicking, tumbling and chasing brought a lot of chuckles. When Zeb got tired, he would climb a giant ash tree in the corner of the yard, search out a comfortable fork, and sleep without interference. Zeb still liked to come into the house. My father complained about him being underfoot.

"Get that darn 'coon out of here!"

"OK, Dad." I responded quickly because my father frequently kicked at the growing raccoon. I worried about it until I noticed that the kicks always missed. He really liked that raccoon.

Zeb's favorite resting place was a cushioned rocking chair on the front porch. In the warm sun, he would sleep there for hours. I would slip up and unceremoniously dump him out of it, then run away as fast as I could.

But his retaliation was swift and sure because Zeb could run faster than I could. Growling fiercely—but using neither tooth nor claw—he would slap me on the legs with his strangely humanlike paws.

We usually wound up tumbling on the grass with the puppy racing around us, barking wildly.

There was a tree with low limbs near the chicken coop. On summer evenings when it was time to roost, many of the hens would fly up and roost on the limbs. Zeb would climb up and walk along the limbs, knocking the chickens off one by one.

Their squawking and flapping always drew the same response from my mother: "Jay, get that 'coon away from my chickens!"

I would get a small switch and start across the yard. Zeb would race across the yard as if terrified and scramble up his favorite tree. Then he would look down innocently as if to say "Who, *me*?"

All I had to do was say, "Come on, 'coon, let's go hunting," and he would join me instantly. We would head for the springhouse, which had a small stream flowing from it. This stream led to a larger creek. There I would turn over rocks and Zeb would pounce on crayfish, tadpoles, frogs and shellfish. Raccoons will eat almost anything. It isn't quite true that they wash their food; I think dunking would be a better description.

Raccoons are good fighters and swimmers. When pursued by a single dog, they may lure him into a deep pool of water and drown the hound.

A neighboring farmer said, "Son, keep that 'coon away from my dog."

The man was not being mean; he was concerned about both the 'coon and the dog. Some people feel very strongly about their pets. He was trying to prevent hard feelings between good neighbors.

As the weather became colder, the back porch became unsatisfactory for Zeb. He burrowed under the porch until he reached the base

of the fireplace chimney, and there he established his lair. Since the fireplace was our main source of heat, the fire was never allowed to go out; my father banked it every night and started it up first thing next morning. Our raccoon's choice showed his intelligence—and probably made him the most comfortable member of the household.

Raccoons do not hibernate, but during bitterly cold spells, Zeb would sleep until the weather moderated. With the coming of spring, he was a grown raccoon. Most of the antics ceased, and he started sleeping all day and roaming at night.

I was concerned about his change of habits although they were quite natural. A few people have an antipathy toward these clean, intelligent animals because some of them become rabid.

Zeb's favorite place was a cushioned rocking chair on the front porch.

In addition to this, I felt he would soon leave home. This bothered me because raccoon pelts were bringing a good price at the time.

Raccoons are attracted by bright objects. Some trappers would bore a hole in a log in or along a stream and put a white button in the bottom. They would then toe four nails into the hole at a slant, allowing room for the 'coon to reach in for the button. Once he grabbed the button, he could not remove his paw. I hope this cruel practice has stopped with the decreased demand for pelts.

I missed his company during the day. Since he was reluctant to go, I put a rope around his neck and took him exploring with Brutus. We flushed a rabbit, and Brutus was off like a shot. I dropped the rope to watch the rabbit's tactics (Brutus always lost).

When the commotion was over, Zeb had disappeared. I was not unduly worried because he could untie a granny knot at will.

But the next day he did not show up. I found him hanging in his favorite ash tree. He had climbed the tree for privacy, or to look for birds' eggs. The rope had become entangled, and in his efforts to free it, he had lost his footing. The knot had slipped to the nape of his neck, out of reach to untie or gnaw through. He was dead. I had, in effect, hanged my favorite pet.

After all these years, the guilt lingers. ❖

Jeff Davis Loved Grandma's Hair

By Esther K. Schulz

As Grandma stepped down from the surrey, she removed her hat, lifted her head and, with eyes closed, took in great gulps of our fresh Michigan country air. "Ah, heavenly," she said. "After that sooty train ride across the country, this is divine." The moment I saw her silvery white hair, I called out, "Grandma, quick! Your hat! Put it back on! If Jeff Davis sees you …"

But my warning came too late. Jeff's raucous cawing announced that he had seen Grandma's lovely white hair and was circling for a landing. Unless she put on her hat quickly, he would drop smack on her head and start rooting around in her hair with his beak. And he wasn't at all gentle when tackling anything white.

Jeff was my big brother's pet crow. Win had raised the bird from a chick. The little thing had fallen from its nest high in a tree. Win named the crow Jefferson Davis; he never said why, but the name stuck.

Every time he saw her; he wanted her to let down her hair!

Jeff responded whenever we called—except now. I yelled at him, but he had eyes only for that pure silvery hair crowning Grandma's head. He landed—right on top.

Grandma's hands flew to her head, but not soon enough to fend off Jeff's landing. Her startled expression and flailing arms sent us into gales of laughter.

"It's only Jeff Davis, Grandma. He won't hurt you. He just wants to investigate your hair." I walked to her and lifted my arms. "Come on, Jeff. Off. You'll have a chance to get at Grandma's hair later."

I brushed him off, but he flew right back to her shoulder. He made a gurgling noise in his throat—his conversation voice, I called it. He pushed his beak through her hair, all the time babbling close to her ear. She stood still.

"He thinks your white hair sits on top of your head just for him to play in, Grandma."

Our grandma was very patient and tolerant with Jeff's antics. But one day she had to scold him. "Jefferson Davis," she said, "stop that rooting. You're making perfect shambles of my hair."

"But Grandma," I said, "Jeff *likes* you. I think he is trying to tell you something. Like maybe he can't leave your hair alone. It is so beautiful. He's never seen anything like it. I've never seen anything so lovely either."

"Oh 'shaw!" Grandma said. "Wherever did your brother get this bird anyway?"

"Win found him down in the pasture. The poor thing fell out of his nest. Too wee to fly."

"Nothing wrong with his flying now," Grandma said. "And he seems to be full of tricks."

One of Jeff's tricks was swooping down on the flock of white chickens to make them squawk. What a racket! And every wash day, he'd hop along the clothesline and try to pull out the clothespins—but only the pins fastening the sheets, pillowcases and white underclothes. Whenever I wore a white hair ribbon, Jeff

hopped on my head and pulled and tugged at the bow until the ribbon dropped off.

"I guess white hurts his eyes or something," Win said. "He sure doesn't like it."

All that summer, every time Grandma stepped outdoors, Jeff flew to her shoulder to root around in her hair. He'd pull out a hairpin, fly with it to the roof of the barn and sit there, holding the pin with one foot and cackling as if he knew a big joke.

Grandma wore old-fashioned, two-pronged aluminum pins that white-haired ladies wore years ago. That kind slipped out of her hair easily. Poor Grandma! "Really, this business has to stop," Grandma said one day. "I won't have any pins left unless I can persuade Jeff to give them back."

"Why don't you just tell him?" I said. "He

understands everything we say. Just say, 'Give that back, Jeff.' I bet it would work." Of course, it didn't.

"I'll fix that rascal," Grandma said. The next time we walked down the lane to the mailbox, Grandma slipped only one pin in at the bun at the back of her neck. As usual, Jeff flew to her shoulder and hunted until he found that one pin. He yanked it out.

But before he could fly off with the pin in his beak, Grandma's hair fell down her back. It hung all the way down past her waist. Jeff was so surprised that he hopped up and down on her shoulder, then dropped to the ground. He sat there with the pin still in his beak, eyeing that thick, long hair. He went through his nodding routine, stretching his neck out and back.

Grandma bent over him and said quietly, "All right, Jefferson Davis, give me that hairpin, or I'll never let my hair down again."

That crazy, stunned crow didn't move. He just stood there and eyed her steadily. She took hold of the hairpin; Jeff let go without a caw, flew to her shoulder and sat there, shoving his beak and forth through her hair.

After that, Grandma put only one hairpin in her bun whenever we were outside. Jeff always pulled out the pin the minute he flew to her shoulder, then gave it up without any of his usual protest. Nor did he try to fly to the barn roof to hide the pin. He acted as if Grandma's hair fell down just for him. He made those gurgling noises in his throat. It became a favorite game.

"I guess he's happy. I do think he's trying to say 'thank you,' Grandma," I told her.

In September, before Grandma left for her home out West, my father ordered the barn reroofed. Under two loose shingles, the roofers found 10 aluminum hairpins pushed as far up under the shingles as they would go. The men shook their heads in wonder.

But we knew how they came to be there. It was all because Jeff Davis had a love affair with Grandma's white hair. ❖

Preacher and the Frog

By Joan Weston

Having to grow up in the middle of nowhere and having few toys and no money seemed like terrible disadvantages at the time, but we entertained ourselves with Mother Nature's animals—and lived to laugh about it.

One spring day when I was 13, my brother told me there were "millions of baby frogs in the pond." Later that evening, we went to the pond with buckets. Both of us dipped up a generous supply of baby frogs and put them in Grandma's rain barrel outside the kitchen door.

A day or two later, when we came home from school, we found the barrel overturned and our frogs gone. Grandpa had found them, and we were told not to bring any more baby frogs from the pond.

He didn't say we couldn't have a big frog, though. We found a gigantic bullfrog and put it in the rain barrel. Grandma dipped the wash water carefully. Grandpa didn't find it, and we kept the frog in the barrel all summer. Every day we carried the frog around and played with it, and then we tucked it back into the barrel.

One hot summer afternoon, I was playing with the frog and I took it into the house. By the time my eyes became accustomed to the darkness inside the house, I was halfway across the kitchen—and there sat the preacher!

He spoke to me. "Hello, Joan, what do you have there?"

It was too late to escape. "A frog."

"Does your frog have a name?" he asked.

"Rumpelstiltskin," I answered.

"May I see your frog?" he asked, holding out his hand.

The preacher was a city fellow, and it soon became obvious that he had never held a cold, clammy, live frog. He certainly didn't know he was supposed to cup his fingers around the frog, and before he had a chance to recover from his first shock, the frog jumped in his lap and onto the floor. The preacher yelled, jumped and fell onto the floor beside his overturned chair.

My mother and aunt started yelling at me to "Get that frog out of the house!" and Grandma rushed out of the pantry to help the fallen minister to his feet.

The frog was as excited as everyone else, and it hopped across the kitchen floor in big leaps while I, on my hands and knees, tried to catch it.

I finally caught the frog under the table, grabbing it with both hands. As I headed out the back door, I heard the preacher say, "I didn't know it was alive!"

I hope he didn't think I would play with a dead frog! ❖

1933 *The Country Home*, House of White Birches nostalgia archives

My Son's Loving Care

By N.E. Chapman

W hen I gaze at the photograph of my son Roy, then age 14, feeding his baby squirrel with a doll bottle while his brother Ronald, 12, watched, that event of many years ago seems like it just happened. On that Saturday morning, Roy came home from an overnight camping trip with his Boy Scout troop. My eyes widened. "Roy! What's that wiggling in your shirt pocket?"

"It's Tinsey."

"Tinsey? Don't you mean Tiny?"

"No, Mom. I named her Tinsey," Roy said, removing the tiny, hairless creature from his pocket.

"It's a baby squirrel. Its eyes aren't open yet so it must be a newborn," his father said. "Son, where did you find it?"

"In the woods. I looked all over for a nest, but couldn't find one." Roy looked at me with pleading eyes while the baby nibbled on his fingers. "I couldn't leave her all alone without her mother."

"Of course you couldn't," I said. "The little thing is hungry. I'll go to the variety store and get a doll bottle."

1929 P&G soap ad, House of White Birches nostalgia archives

When I returned, I filled the doll bottle with warm milk and gave it to my son. Roy held the bottle while Tinsey nursed. Ronald said, "It's so tiny. I guess that's why you named her Tinsey." Roy nodded.

"Son, it'll be your responsibility to care for Tinsey," his father said. "Do you understand?" Roy nodded again. He placed a towel in a box for the squirrel. Before and after school, he fed her from the doll bottle. While he was in school, I cared for her.

A month later, Tinsey's black eyes opened and she developed a reddish brown coat. She recognized the bottle and learned to hold it while nursing. She knew Roy and seemed to enjoy his cuddling.

During the next six months, we watched Tinsey grow. When she felt hungry, she sat on her haunches in front of the refrigerator, chattering and scolding to be fed.

"I have some fruit and veggies for you," Roy would say. He filled a bowl with food, then sat on the floor, feeding her.

Each day when Roy came in from school, he'd call, "Tinsey, I'm home." She'd run to him and climb up into his arms, and he'd cuddle and stroke her.

Then I began missing things, like my thimble and spools of thread. Roy knew Tinsey was hiding them. When he caught her chewing on chair legs, he picked her up and gently shook her. "Tinsey, don't be a bad girl." Her black eyes held his for a moment, then she jumped down and scurried away, looking for something else to do.

That evening when Roy's father came home, I looked at him and our son. "Tinsey

has become destructive. She's chewing up things. You two will have to keep her outside in a cage."

"She'll get lonesome out there all alone," Roy protested.

The author's son Roy (right), feeding his baby squirrel, Tinsey. His brother, Ronald, is watching. Their joy is plainly etched on their faces.

"She won't," his father said. "We'll put a wheel in the cage and other things she can play with."

"She might get out and run away," Ronald stated with concern.

After the cage had been finished, Roy placed Tinsey in it. Each day after school, he said, "Come on, we'll play a few minutes; then I'll have to return you to the cage."

But Roy soon learned that Tinsey found ways to get out of the cage. Each time, he would mend the hole, catch her and return her to the cage. After that happened several times, his father said, "Roy, that squirrel should be turned loose."

"No, Dad. I can't give her up."

That day when Roy came home, he found the cage empty. Then he spotted Tinsey on his neighbor's back porch roof. At that moment, Mrs. Childers, the neighbor, stepped out through her back porch doorway.

Her screams brought Roy running. Flabbergasted, he saw Tinsey clinging to the woman's head. She screeched like a police whistle, her eyes bulging with terror. Mrs. Childers walked slowly to the kitchen with Roy trailing behind her. He got a head of lettuce from the refrigerator and waved it. Tinsey moved to the hysterical woman's shoulder.

"Get this beast off me!" she howled.

Roy waved the lettuce, coaxing Tinsey. She leaped from the woman's shoulder and Roy grabbed her. Once freed, the woman slowly regained her dignity. Later, they laughed about it.

When I learned about that episode, I realized Roy should release Tinsey. After school that day, I hugged him. "Honey, you must take Tinsey back to her woods. It's not right to cage her. She needs to be free."

"But, Mom, she might starve."

"She won't. Her instinct for survival will help her find food. Besides, there are other squirrels she can play with. I'll go with you."

Late that afternoon, we traveled to the woods. Roy held Tinsey and stroked her. He looked at me with eyes that said it was one of the hardest things he'd ever had to do. He caressed Tinsey, then set her on the ground. She looked up at him and climbed back into his arms.

"Tinsey, I'll never forget you." He set her down again and gave her a small shove. "Go on, you're free," he choked. "Be good, and don't jump on another lady's head."

Tinsey looked at her hero for a moment. Then she ran to a tree and scampered up. "Goodbye, Tinsey," Roy said through tears he no longer could hold back.

I placed my arm around his shoulder. "Come on, son. Your brother can toss a few balls so you can practice batting."

I brushed a tear away when I remembered how sad Roy felt when we returned from the woods that day. But he had learned a lesson— that we should admire and respect all wild creatures, but it isn't a good idea to make pets of them. I knew Roy would never forget Tinsey because he had that picture of his brother and him feeding her from the doll bottle. ❖

Squeaky

By Ruby Sillin

The most unusual pet we ever had as children growing up was a wild groundhog. My father was cutting firewood early in the spring when he found a little groundhog crawling around, perhaps looking for its mother. My dad had a  soft spot; he picked the little thing up, put it in his pocket and brought it home.

My sister Edna Mae took it in her care right away, feeding it and keeping it warm. It ate lettuce and carrots and potatoes.

Dad gave it a drawer in an old chest of drawers. That was his place. He would crawl into the drawer from the back, and if we opened the drawer, we would get a scolding from him.

If we dropped a piece of paper on the floor, it became his, and he would take it into the drawer for his bed.

My sister Edna Mae took him outside a lot during the summer. She took him on walks with her, and as soon as she came in, he wanted in, too. She named him Squeaky, and where she was, Squeaky was too. When all three of us girls sat on the sofa, he always went to Edna Mae.

Squeaky grew to a good, healthy size. He stayed with us for about two years. Then, early one spring day, he just took off.

My dad told Edna Mae that Squeaky had gone to find a mate so he could have his own family. Edna Mae was brokenhearted anyway. ❖

Groundhog Day

By Mary Baxter Carroll

A groundhog's shadow has nothing to do with weather forecasting. It's merely a superstition, and a fun one. This varmint may hibernate until early March, depending upon how cold it is and how much snow covers the burrow.

Until gardens and wild plants grow, these rodents have a difficult time finding enough to eat. They often live close to or beneath farm buildings. Two to six young are born in April, their eyes opening two to three weeks later. They make good pets.

We once had a pet woodchuck. He was so tiny that Mother fed him a formula of creamed cereal using an eyedropper. His first nest was a quart berry basket, but it quickly became too small for the fast-growing ball of fur.

Chucky was playful and impish. He had a fuzzy, bewhiskered face, and his shiny shoe-button eyes were ever on the alert for food, frolics and fights. He liked an audience, and he liked to hear us laugh.

But our cat, Felix, didn't think he was funny. That pesky woodchuck liked to sleep in Felix's warm box behind the kitchen stove. Chucky was sneaky, too. He would wait until Felix fell asleep, then sneak up and take a quick nip at the cat's tail before scooting off lickety-split, out of sight and out of reach of Felix's unsheathed claws. Felix never was fast enough on the draw.

Chucky most certainly did not like to be disturbed while he was snoozing. He would chatter angrily, his short tail sticking straight up. He would bite anyone, even the dog, who dared come too near.

We had an inside privy. It wasn't pretty or fancy, but it did have toilet paper. It wasn't long before Chucky discovered this cozy spot, including the toilet paper and its fine nest-making qualities.

During our absence one Sunday morning, he proceeded to carry his newfound treasure, streamer after streamer, beneath a porch cupboard. Our furry rascal unfurled every bit of the fresh roll that had been placed in the "inner sanctum" that very morning.

Soon his areas of exploration widened—much to our relief and his pleasure. Chucky moved outdoors to quarters beneath the kitchen, the porch, the barns and woodpile. He also found access beneath the chicken house, but this disturbed the hens. This potential abode was eliminated in short order when Grandpa placed a barrier of chicken wire embedded in concrete around the base of the coop.

Chucky liked the root cellar, too, because of the delicious vegetables and fruits stored there. Should the door be left ajar, he was sure to notice … an invitation to a banquet! He would go hog wild, sampling everything available, including turnips and onions!

Once he got caught in an old, rusty trap set along the stone wall by one of the neighbors' boys. Thankfully, Chucky was found shortly after this mishap. The trap was not too powerful, but it was strong enough to break the skin on his left hind foot. It healed, but a plainly visible scar remained across the top of his foot.

He was snoopy, sassy, a pest and not much good for anything—but we loved him.

As Chucky grew, so did his world. He migrated to the upper lot his first autumn. He made a hole beneath the oak overhanging the glen. The following spring, he still acknowledged us, but he never again allowed us to touch him. Off and on during the summer, he would answer Daddy's whistle from across the field, or watch us from a respectable distance.

The last time we saw Chucky was the next spring, when he was 2 years old. We were on our way to school, across from the sawmill. One warm morning, we saw him sitting on the bank at the lip of a fresh hole, and he chattered at us. We knew it was Chucky by the scar on his left hind foot. ❖

Our Big Orphan Annie

By Alice Cundiff

Like many Central Alberta farmers of the early 1930s, Earl and Buelah Cundiff, my husband's parents, had suffered crop failure because of hail, drought and winds. Hoping to better themselves, they moved from the Haynes district east of Lacombe to Fort Assiniboine in the northern part of the province. Homesteading back then was grueling and often discouraging. But an unexpected and unusual pet brought enjoyment and laughter as well as frustration.

While walking to get the cows for evening milking, the Cundiffs discovered a moose calf, about one day old, lying in the grass. Her mother had met with an unfortunate sudden death.

Earl carried the young moose partway home. When he put her down on wobbly legs, she followed them, showing no fear or apprehension. "Orphan Annie" settled in quickly and seemed to feel right at home. The homestead was 20 miles from Fort Assiniboine, and there was not a lot of cleared land, so Annie did not feel that far from her natural habitat.

An intelligent and lovable animal, Annie was never restrained in any way; she had complete freedom.

At first she was fed cow's milk from a bottle using a lamb's nipple. Within a few days she was drinking from a pail, and she quickly became strong and playful. The young moose loved strawberries, bread, pastry—almost anything except meat.

Annie generally disliked women and children—except for Buelah. A strong bond developed between them. When berry-picking time came, Annie loved to go along. While Buelah picked strawberries, Annie would take a dip in the lake or go for a run, checking every few minutes to make sure she had not been left behind. She'd also eat some berries if she could get away with it. When she could not find Buelah (who sometimes hid from her), she would begin a lonesome cry as if calling her mother.

Annie also had a sense of humor of sorts. She loved to sneak into the house and jump up and down on the bed as though it were a trampoline. Also, she could walk by the dog 50 times, ignoring him completely, and the next time, whack him, first with a front hoof and then a hind one. Old Ring howled blue murder while Annie made an easy escape over the fence. Ring always gave chase, but the ritual was sure to be repeated.

One of her favorite escapades was to jump the fence into the pigpen or corral and chase the pigs and calves away so she could eat their feed. No matter how many poles were added, she just kept going over. Finally the Cundiffs had to take turns staying in the pen at feeding time to keep Annie away while the animals ate.

Annie developed another strategy that was seldom successful. With her eye on a particular cow, she would walk slowly and quietly across the corral until she was directly behind it. Then, kneeling down, she would thrust her mouth between the cow's hind legs, hoping to enjoy an afternoon snack of warm milk. The cow, who did not like her much anyway, would casually walk away, leaving poor Annie to look for another target.

The Cundiffs' nearest neighbor was 4 miles away, and when Buelah went visiting there, Annie always tagged along. After crying plaintively outside the house for a while, she would lie down and wait quietly until it was time to go home.

An intelligent and lovable animal, Annie was never restrained in any way; she had complete freedom to roam as she wished. Sometimes she was gone for a few hours, sometimes all day. But when her name was called a few times, she would come trotting home.

On these occasions, she received a reward, such as a piece of bread, a pancake or a pan of milk. Bread was one of her favorite treats, and she was trained to jump onto Earl's shoulder to get it.

Photograph by Betty George © 2008 sxc.com

Annie had spent about two years with the Cundiffs when one day she failed to respond to their calls. Earl and Buelah were saddened to discover that, like her mother, Annie's life had been ended abruptly by a bullet.

Despite being a nuisance sometimes, Annie also brought much enjoyment, and she was greatly missed.

Remembering Orphan Annie still brings laughter to Mrs. Cundiff, who now is widowed and lives in Abbotsford, B.C. ❖

Petunia and My Other Pets

By Wayne Giacomo

Growing up during the Depression years was a hardship for many, but for me, it was a privilege. Having no brothers or sisters with whom to play nor money for toys or entertainment, I reverted to nature for my pleasure. I had many pets during those years—dogs, cats, horses, chickens and pigeons. I was granted the privilege of naming all the farm animals. Usually I named them after flowers; the cows, for example, had such names as Rose, Pansy, Daisy, Fern, Violet and Lily.

Besides my domesticated animals and feathered friends, I had wild ones as well.

For instance, there were Petunia and Honeysuckle. One day my dad and I were taking several sacks of wheat to my uncle's farm to get it fanned before planting time. We were taking the team and wagon.

Petunia had a broad stripe and was easily tamed.

There was a gate to open before we entered my uncle's pasture. When I jumped from the wagon to open it, I heard rustling in the leaves in the road ditch. Looking down into the ditch, I saw a mother skunk and her five young ones. I said, "Oh, Dad, can I have one for a pet?"

He replied, "You will get sprayed."

That did not deter me at all. By this time, the mother skunk was rambling off through the pasture. Dad told me that if I was determined to catch one, I should pick it up by the tail so it could not spray.

I came out of the ditch with one of the babies. I dropped it into the wagon. It tried to escape, but the steep sides of the high-wheeled wagon bed kept it in. Eventually it crawled in among the sacks of wheat to hide.

When we returned from my uncle's, I immediately started to tame my new pet.

Petunia had a broad stripe and was easily tamed. My dad told me I'd have to have her de-scented by the vet.

A few days later, we had to call the vet out to look at a sick horse. While he was there, I asked him how much it would cost to de-scent Petunia. He told me it would cost about $4. I put her in a small cage so the vet could take her back to his office. He called in a day or two with some good news. Petunia had no scent glands. She was naturally de-scented. I had never heard of this before, nor have I heard of it since.

I was very happy, though, because the operation would have been very risky for her. Petunia became a most affectionate pet. She loved to be rubbed, and she would curl up in my lap and take a snooze, just like a kitten.

I kept Petunia for four or five years. One day when I took her bread and milk, I found her dead in her bed. I buried her in the back of the garden beside her sister. For a long time after that I put bouquets of wildflowers on her grave.

Then there was Willie Mutton. Yes, Willie was a sheep. We had a neighbor named Charlie whose nickname was Roebuck. Roebuck raised sheep.

One cold day in early spring, Roebuck came to our house with something draped over his arm. It was a new male lamb. Its mother would not claim it, so Roebuck brought it to me.

My mom put it in a box behind the old kitchen range and gave it a bottle of warm milk. Within an hour he was following me all over the kitchen. From that time on, he was my constant companion. He was nosy and intelligent, and he was a troublemaker. I had to walk a mile and a half to school. He would walk part of the way with me, but when he got to the pasture gate near the main road, he would turn around and head for home. In the evening he would watch for me. When he saw me coming, he would come bounding toward me as if to say, "I knew you'd be here soon."

I learned to love him very much, but my parents didn't seem to share that love. Mother had geese. While I was away at school, Willie and the geese were companions in mischief. One day they found Mom's truck patch down by the creek. The green beans were already to the top of the poles. The geese stripped the beans as high as they could reach, and Willie stood on his hind legs and finished stripping the rest of the way. There were no pole beans for my mother to can that year. Needless to say, that didn't go over very well.

Willie grew up to be 2 years old. He still followed me to the gate each day and met me each evening. One day Willie didn't meet me. I ran home as fast as I could. When I told Mom about Willie not meeting me, she looked at me and said, "Willie won't be with you anymore. When the truck came this morning to take the calves to the stockyard, your dad put Willie in the truck and sent him also."

My life was shattered. I cried for days. I could not understand why Dad would do that without any warning. To this day I have not forgotten it.

Another of my pets was Hootin' Annie. Annie was a screech owl, and she was a beautiful, darling little pet.

My dad and I were rabbit hunting one day, and the dogs ran a rabbit into a standing hollow tree. My dad stuck his arm into the tree to see if he could reach the rabbit. He pulled the rabbit out of the hole, all right, but as he did, something else latched onto his hand.

He reached back into the tree and came out with the little owl. We took her home and put her in a rabbit cage.

Annie became quite gentle. However, she also was not a favorite pet of my parents.

On summer nights when we tried to sleep, Annie would sing to us. If you've never heard the plaintive cry of a screech owl, you have missed something. With no electricity and no air conditioning, we had to have the windows open. The noise was quite disturbing. One morning I found the door to Annie's cage open. Annie was gone. I assume she went back to her old haunts in the woods.

I had many other wild creatures as pets. There was Inky, a 6-foot blacksnake we kept in our corncrib; Slinky, a fox cub I could lead around like a puppy; Coony, a raccoon; and Popeye, a crow.

I vividly remember how I got each of them and the story of their lives with me. I still love birds and animals and have always had pets through the years.

My last wild bird was Jimmy, a crow. Jimmy died last summer, apparently from old age. I had him for about 10 years.

With all of my experiences with so many different animals, I came to realize that nothing can compare to God's wonderful creatures. ❖

Coonie

By Richard E. Schillinger

In 1956, my folks built a new house in the rural area of Caledonia, N.Y., south of Rochester. My Uncle Bill was on the way to our house when he came across a baby raccoon wandering by the side of the road. Its mother had been killed trying to cross the road.

The baby was very small; in fact, its eyes were not yet open. Uncle Bill gave the baby raccoon to me to raise. I named him Coonie. I bottle-fed him with a baby-doll bottle, mixing a little milk of magnesia with the raw cow's milk to help him digest it.

Coonie grew and became somewhat tame. I fed him bread broken up in milk in a metal hog pan. (He liked the crusts best and would eat them first.) He also liked some vegetables, especially tomatoes, corn, zucchini and watermelon. We kept another hog pan of fresh water in his cage for drinking and for washing or moistening his food.

I would take him out of the large cage and play with him. He also liked to play with our beagle dog, Pep-C. They wrestled until one or the other got too rough or tired and walked away.

Coonie became quite large, about 30 pounds, and we had to handle him with thick, heavy-duty gloves. He loved to ride on my shoulder or my father's shoulder while we walked around the yard.

He loved to get up on the white board fence that surrounded our garden. He'd wait there until I picked him some cherry tomatoes. Then he would take them in his paws and eat them as the juice ran down his chin and onto his belly. He would lick the juice from his belly before accepting another tomato. Coonie delighted our family and visitors with his antics and eating habits.

I kept him until late the following spring, and then I left the cage door open so he could come and go as he pleased. Coonie would come back and sleep and eat in the cage for a couple of weeks, and then we wouldn't see him for awhile. But when the cherry tomatoes ripened, he would come at dusk and sit on the fence and make a calling noise until I came out and picked tomatoes for him.

The next year, when he was 2 years old, we sometimes saw him along the rear of our property, but that was all.

Coonie was a great pet who provided lots of entertainment for me and my family. He was part of our Good Old Days. ❖

The Orphan Mouse Caper

By Livingstone Lathan Jr.

The railroad tracks north of town are gone now, but back in the 1930s when I was growing up in the little village of Clinton in southeastern Michigan, the big steam locomotives of the New York Central line pulled their passenger and freight cars through town daily. Our home was only a block from the tracks, and the railroad right-of-way was one of our favorite places to play, made even more alluring by the fact that it was off-limits.

One early summer's day, I was poking along the tracks about a half-mile north of town when I spotted a nest of field mice. There were four of them, and they were practically brand new, hairless and not having their eyes open yet. Of course, no 10-year-old boy worth his salt could pass up a prize of this magnitude, so I carefully eased the little mice into the pocket of my knickers and headed for home.

My mother was less than enthusiastic over my find. However, I knew how soft-hearted she was, and after considerable teasing and a really inspired narrative about how their parents had undoubtedly been killed by a speeding locomotive and how the poor things would die a slow, agonizing death of starvation, Mother agreed to let me keep them until they were old enough to fend for themselves.

I eased the little mice into the pocket of my knickers and headed for home.

The only condition Mother attached was that I was to be solely responsible for their care and feeding, as she was most certainly not going to have anything to do with them.

One of my most cherished memories is of my mother holding those naked little mice in her hand and feeding them with an eyedropper. I don't recall what kid of concoction Mother fed those mice, but they certainly thrived on it. In no time at all, they had their eyes open and had grown beautiful soft coats of gray hair.

They were cute as a bug's ear, but they were getting to the point where they were outgrowing their shoebox home. Mother warned me of the dire consequences should any of my little wards escape into the house. I assured her that there was absolutely no way in the world this could possibly happen, as I always kept the lid on the box secured by a strong rubber band.

It was early Sunday morning when we discovered the mice had escaped. We were just sitting down to breakfast when my dad noticed Pat, our Irish setter, wasn't at her usual station by my chair, trying to mooch a share of my breakfast. Pat was curled up in the far corner of the kitchen with that "Boy, am I in trouble now" look on her face. When Dad called to her, she reluctantly came to his chair and very gently deposited a small mouse at his feet.

The mouse was slightly damp but otherwise none the worse for wear. Pat was between litters of puppies, and she had a strong mothering instinct. She trotted back to the corner of the kitchen and returned with another one of "her babies." This was repeated until all four of the little mice were by the table. Pat was obviously pleased with herself to think that she had managed to acquire a new litter without any of the usual discomforts associated with motherhood.

As soon as Dad stopped laughing and got Mother calmed down, he suggested that this might be an appropriate time to return the mice to their natural habitat. We had planned to leave for church right after breakfast, but Mother said she was sure God would understand if we used the time to see to it that four of His little creatures were provided with a nice home in the country.

After making sure the mice were secure in the shoebox, we all piled in our 1935 Hudson Terraplane. We had intended to leave Pat home, but she raised such a fuss when she saw we were leaving with her newly adopted offspring that Dad let her come along.

We drove several miles out into the country and stopped next to a small meadow near woods. It was a tranquil-looking spot and seemed to be an ideal location for the little orphans to start their new life.

As I gently placed the shoebox on the ground and removed the cover, all four of the little mice tumbled out and scurried away into the tall grass. Dad assured me that they would be much better off here where they were meant to be. I knew he was right, of course, and I felt a sense of pride mixed with sadness to see them leave the nest and strike out on their own.

We drove home in silence. Pat sniffed the empty shoebox and gave me a reproachful look. Fortunately, little boys and Irish setters seem to have the ability to recover fairly rapidly from disappointments, and in a few days, the orphan mice were just another pleasant memory. ❖

My Pet, Foxy

By Margaret Miller Cantrell

In the 1940s when we lived in Waterville, Minn., my dad, Clyde Miller, brought home a baby fox one night. We named him Foxy.

We soon learned Foxy was a one-person animal. The only time he really liked Mama was when she was fixing meat, as she would give Foxy some. I could pet him a little, but my younger sister, Marie, had to walk with her hands in the air. Foxy liked to nip her fingers.

Daddy taught Foxy to jump through a hoop. He would give Foxy a treat each time. The bowl of treats was always on the piano. Sometimes we would hear a clatter and run to see what had happened. Foxy would be sitting on the floor with treats all around him, but looking so very innocent.

Marie and I soon learned to keep shoes, socks and toys picked up, as Foxy would take them to his den, the basement, and chew them completely up.

My cousin Lewis Smith lived in Morristown. He often visited us, and soon Foxy would do tricks for him as well as Daddy. When we moved to Washington, Daddy gave Foxy to Lewis.

My cousin Ike worked at a meat market. Lewis would put Foxy on a leash and take him to the meat market to get a bone. Then Lewis would lay the leash over Foxy's back and send him home.

It didn't take the neighborhood dogs long to learn to cross over to the other side when Foxy had a bone. If a dog tried to take it, Foxy would lay his bone down, whip the dog, pick his bone up and continue on his way.

One night when everyone was gone, someone turned Foxy loose. We never saw him again. He will always be in our memories as the most unusual pet we ever had. ❖

Remembering My Childhood Pets

By Lucille Moreau

I remember the farm we lived on during my childhood days. We lived in a green-shingled house with seven rooms and a very large yard with an old barn in the rear of the yard. On the side of the barn was a chicken coop. We owned 45 hens and roosters. I loved to feed them corn. They would run over to the food the minute it was thrown into the coop. That food was always gone in no time, and I would run into the house for more. Those chickens really got more than their share of chow.

We also owned a dog, Mitsie. The first time we saw Mitsie, he was poor and thin, and just a month old. We knew that Mitsie was a male, but my mother said that I was the one who named him, and since I kept saying Mitsie, the name kind of stuck. It sure didn't take long for Mom to fatten that animal up. It seemed that every time we saw her, she was feeding Mitsie.

> *It gave me a really good feeling to hear Pee Wee singing.*

I loved the color of Mitsie's fur; he was black, white, gray and brown, all mixed together. Even as a puppy, he always looked like an old man because the gray color caught my eye the most.

My brothers used to take in lame birds, and one day, Herman came to stay with us for a while. Herman was a gray-and-white pigeon whose leg was injured, and he was a bit blind. He kept running into things and tripping on his lame leg.

My brothers nursed Herman back to health, and I think they even cured his blindness by feeding him cod liver oil. Soon he was just like part of the family. Soon thereafter, we let him go free.

One bird, a tiny sparrow, also stands tall in my memory. We found him in a trash can one morning just after breakfast. He was chirping very weakly and had an injured wing. We made a bed for him out of a cardboard box filled with cotton. He was so tiny that we named him Pee Wee.

It was an unusually chilly day for the middle of spring, so we put the heat on that night and kept Pee Wee beside the stove. The next morning, Pee Wee was weaker than ever. Still, we all had hope, and I think that hope is what brought that little bird strength, because that night, he was hopping all over the kitchen. Soon his wing was healed.

He stayed with us for two weeks more. Then we knew the day had come to let Pee Wee go free. He stayed in my hands as I carried him into the field. My heart broke for a moment, but then I thought how glad Pee Wee must have felt to have his freedom at last.

Exactly five days later, on a Sunday morning, our little sparrow was back, perched on the clothesline and chirping away to let the world know that he was happy. I knew it was Pee Wee; my dad had been painting one day when Pee Wee was staying with us, and a drop of green paint had fallen onto his side. Now, there was Pee Wee, perched on Mom's clothesline, standing tall and proud, the only sparrow with green paint on his feathers.

Every day from then on, Pee Wee came to visit with us. It really gave me a good feeling to hear him singing. We always left food out on the grass for him, and he and other birds would feast on it. Pee Wee came to visit us for about a year and a half. After that, I missed him terribly.

I never knew why he never came back. There could have been so many reasons. Thoughts would run through my head; perhaps he was injured, or perhaps he was even dead. I always hoped that wherever he was, God would take care of him. I never forgot that tiny bird.

Today he still stands out in my memory, especially since my niece found an injured sparrow just last week. The strange part of it was that on his side was a faint color of green. It is impossible that it was Pee Wee—birds don't live that long—but I like to think that it was.

I had many good times during my childhood. My sister also was an animal lover, and she always brought in stray cats—Blacky, Snooks, Snowball and, of course, Greyhound. Greyhound was a large, ugly gray cat. He was mean and vicious, so we kept him out in the barn inside a little chicken-wire fence. After a while, though, we had to put him down in the cellar because he was very good at catching mice. With all our cats, we very rarely saw a mouse around our place.

Yes, the green-shingled house, the tall pines in the back yard, the long grass blowing in the fields, the old barn, the swing my dad made, the cookouts we used to have in the open ground, the fireflies, and all the animal friends we had are very precious memories that I will keep forever. ❖

A Snake Named Oscar

By Linnie Meeder

My favorite childhood pet, growing up the fourth of nine kids on a Pennsylvania dairy farm, was a garter snake I named Oscar. I had to keep him a big secret because my mother was terrified of snakes and would faint whenever she saw one.

Oscar went everywhere with me, even to school, in my pocket. One day I didn't notice that Oscar had crawled out of my pocket until all the other girls started screaming and jumping on top of their desks. Our teacher yelled, "Which of you boys brought a snake into school?" so I jumped on top of my desk too.

During recess, one of the boys came up to me and told me he had hid Oscar in a hole in a tree for me and covered him with his handkerchief. As soon as school ended, I rushed out and was happy to find Oscar was still there.

I took him home and hid him in my dresser—a huge mistake, because Mom had done laundry, and she fainted when she found him. That's when Dad made Oscar a cage and he had to live in the barn. But I took him out every day to play with him. ❖

Farm Friends

Chapter Five

Friends were made where you could find them back in the Good Old Days. That was especially true for farm kids like me who didn't have the luxury of a neighborhood full of other youngsters.

So some of my closest friends were the barnyard buddies I found right there on our small acreage in the Ozark Mountains of southern Missouri.

Horses, calves, piglets, lambs and kids (the kind a goat brings into the world) were always among my farm friends. But I have to say that my favorites were the chicks my Grandma Stamps bought every spring.

Chickens were very important to Grandma. Widowed when my mother was just a baby, Grandma Stamps made a meager amount of "egg money" from her layers and made many a Sunday chicken dinner from her fryers.

For a long time, Grandma's chickens raised chicks the old-fashioned way: Instead of gathering the eggs, a hen was allowed to accumulate a nest-full that she then set upon and soon turned into her very own brood.

Then there was a time when the eggs were gathered into the incubator that was set up in the brooder house. It was almost miraculous when the chicks pecked their way out of the shells.

But then Grandma followed the lead of most of our neighbors and began to buy her chicks rather than hatching them.

As I remember, she sometimes had the chicks delivered by the mailman in large cardboard boxes perforated with air-holes. Other times, if a trip coincided with her chick needs, she bought them from the hardware store in town.

Regardless where Grandma bought them from, I loved playing with the little yellow fuzzballs. I made over them like the mother hen they didn't have. They had me well trained as they peeped their way around the brooder house where we kept them until they were large enough to withstand the rigors of the yard and barn lot.

Uncle Bob, Grandma's bachelor son, took an old tire from a Ford Model T and cut it in half down the middle of the tread. That made two troughs—one for watering the chicks and the other for feeding them.

> *I was young, so the names with which I dubbed them weren't very original.*

I picked two or three of the chicks from each year's lot to call my pets. I chose the runts because otherwise it would be impossible to tell them apart. I was young, so the names with which I dubbed them weren't very original. Peeper, Squeaks, Butterball and Chickadee were among the monikers I chose. I'm sure I used the same names a dozen times over the years.

At the end of the season, Grandma made sure that my pet chicks were among those she sold to neighbors. She told me they were going to their farms to lay eggs and be good pet chickens for them.

I just took her at her word for that.

Farm friends like my pet chicks taught me love and compassion, not to mention responsibility. I also learned about some of the harsher realities of life.

The stories in this chapter will remind you of both the gentle and not-so-gentle lessons of life we learned from our farm friends, some of our favorite pets from the Good Old Days.

—Ken Tate

The Greatest Performance

By Mark Morris

My introduction to the beautiful black-and-white paint was made by my dad as he unloaded her from the truck. "Her name is Cricket. She's an Indian pony. I bought her from the circus." I was puzzled, as I had always ridden or led previously purchased ponies home from the local sale barn. Also, Cricket, standing at 12 hands, was taller than our previous Shetlands and Welshes, both small breeds.

It was almost dark as we watered, fed and bedded her down in the pony shed. I asked to sleep there, as I was sometimes permitted to do, but to my surprise and curiosity, the answer was no. "You can spend more time with her tomorrow," Dad said.

I hardly slept, and I was up early the next morning. At breakfast, Dad told me I would need to bathe Cricket. Then he said, "There are some things you should know about her before you start."

"Why did you get a pony I can't ride?" I blurted out.

I waited by the shed door as Dad led her from the stall. Handing me the lead strap, he told me to look at her eyes. I was taken aback by their cloudy appearance and was shocked when he explained, "Cricket is blind."

"Why did you get a pony I can't ride?" I blurted out. "I don't want her!" He was so surprised by my outburst that he took the lead strap from me and put her back in the stall. He told me to get a bucket of water. After he placed it near Cricket's head, she nuzzled the bucket and then drank normally.

Dad looked thoughtful for a moment. Then he motioned for me to sit down with him on a bale of hay. "We better have a little talk," he said. I didn't know why he said "we"; I already knew who was going to do the talking.

"Maybe I should have let you sleep here," he said. "But now I'll explain why I didn't." He named three of our previous ponies, then quizzed me, "What kind of ponies were they?"

"Shetland," I replied

"Right." Then he asked me to recall some of their traits. I remembered that crowding me in a stall had been a certain Shetland's favorite habit, and that I had to be ever alert for sudden, flat-eared warnings that a kick or bite was coming. Shetlands also thought that a cow kick or backbite while I was trying to mount them might be just the thing to get them the day off.

Dad explained that Indian ponies are gentle and not at all moody. Cricket had been a circus pony, and she had lost her sight either from a disease or from a fungus in her feed or bedding. "She only needs a friend she can trust. You can easily train her to follow your commands," he explained.

Then his tone grew stern: "She's bought and paid for, although I paid more to get her home than she cost. Your job is to take care of her. We will train her this summer and sell her in the fall."

His voice softened as he advised, "Ride her as you did the others, except that you must let her know what to expect at all times. Teach her to respond to touch and knee pressure; use soft-spoken warnings and reassurances. Above all, protect her from surprise; keep her aware of her environment. When leading or riding her, imagine how you yourself would need to be forewarned."

Well, I must admit that I felt a bit ashamed as he ended our little talk.

Again he led Cricket from the stall and told me to bathe her, walk her dry, then stake her out in the pasture to graze. As I started to lead her away, he added: "By the way, I must warn you of a couple of her habits. She is gentle; however, she was a clown's pony and has been taught a couple of things that will need changed.

"Be careful as you bathe her. When you touch her hip, she will kick. It will not be done in anger. She was taught this by having a large ball tossed toward her. A clown would touch her hip just as the ball approached and she would kick with both feet and sail the ball to the top of the Big Top.

"As soon as you become acquainted, you can break her of that by patting her hip, then reprimanding her. Be gentle, but let her know that you do not want her to kick. That's enough. She does have one other quirk, but I'll explain that later."

In a couple of days, I had already begun to love Cricket. We were both learning. She was hesitant and often stumbled as I led her.

I began to spend more time with her as she grazed on the lush summer grass. Often, when I staked her out, I just stayed to pet and talk to her. She began to recognize my voice and gain confidence.

At first, I only warned her of difficult footing when I led her across a ditch or passed an obstruction, but each stumble taught me more. By coaxing, I found that she could traverse almost anything I could.

To put her at ease, I warned her not only of changes in terrain, but also made her aware of nearby objects and people.

After only a few days, I saddled her and began to ride her. It was not much different from leading her; by word, by touch, or by change of pace, I let her know what to expect. Each stumble, I realized, shook her confidence, but as days passed, she placed such complete trust in me that she even trotted at my urging. Even a subtle shift of my body alerted her, and I swear she developed a sixth sense for my concern.

Proud of both our achievements, I was anxious to show Dad. One day I asked him to watch as I saddled and mounted Cricket. We trotted away briskly, then I turned her around and urged her to a gallop.

Dad immediately waved and shouted, "No! Stop! Stop!" He hurried to meet me as I reined to a stop. "Be careful! Remember, I told you she had another quirk I would tell you about later? It's time now, I guess." Cricket has been taught another clown trick, he explained. At a gallop, she would suddenly plant all four feet, drop her head between her legs and send the clown flying. The clown, of course, was an expert tumbler who knew how to land. Dad warned me, "Be alert and hold on. At the first sign that she intends to drop her head, you must yank it up and make her keep going."

For the next few days, I was extra careful, but she was too quick for me. I looked silly, hanging on for dear life as she dumped me, but only my pride was hurt—and she always stood patiently as she waited for me to remount.

After a few weeks, she understood that the rules had changed, and then she became a delight to ride. She was beautiful in action— with head high and bobbing, she just pranced along. We had a great summer together.

One evening in the fall, Dad announced over supper the news that almost broke my heart: "Tomorrow we take Cricket to the sale."

In spite of my pleas, his decision stood. My mood was well reflected by the rainy fall day as I rode Cricket to the sale barn. Once there, I placed her in a stall and gave her a tearful goodbye hug. At the auctioneer's call, she was led out for prospective buyers to examine.

The auctioneer started his chant. However, the bids came too slowly for his impatient harangue. "Show her," he told Dad, whereupon I was directed to ride her a few hundred yards out and back in an area he indicated. With only a hackamore on her, I mounted bareback and trotted her out and slowly turned her around. It had begun to drizzle again as two lines of spectators formed a muddy corridor for us.

I was in no mood to show anybody anything, and it occurred to me that if we hit that mud fast, I might splash it on the bidders. I urged Cricket into a hard gallop as we entered the muddy corridor. I had turned my head to sneak a glance at the results of my conniving when Cricket suddenly planted all four feet and dropped her head between her legs.

We came to a sliding stop, spewing mud all around. Only sheer luck and slick mud saved me from tumbling headfirst into a puddle. Grabbing frantically for her mane, I managed to hold on long enough to pull her head up and slide back into a more sedate riding position.

And you know what? No one winked or scratched his nose. No one touched his hat brim. Not one bid was made on my pony.

How happy I was as I rode Cricket home. I thought Dad would be furious, but he wasn't. He was so proud that I, his son, hadn't been thrown there in front of all those people. (I never had the heart to tell him it was just dumb luck.)

As for the rest of the story—we realize what happened, don't we?

That pony was smart. Thundering through that corridor of people and hearing the murmur of the crowd, she had a flashback. *On with the show!* She was back in the circus, tossing the clown! It was her last performance and, in my opinion, her greatest one of all. ❖

Pretty Boy

By Kathy Wallace

For my eighth birthday, one of my presents was a baby parakeet. We lived in Battle Creek, Mich., at the time, and we went to a parakeet farm to choose one. I chose a *very* young turquoise blue bird. Actually, he was so young that his mother was still hulling and feeding him his seed, so we had to place his seed in a sock and crush it with a hammer so he was able to eat it.

He was guaranteed to talk, and talk he did. The first thing he learned was to whistle. Then we taught him several phrases. When I left for school, as soon as the door closed, he would say, "Kathy's gone to school." He also said, "My name is Pretty Boy. What's yours?" and "Give me sugar" and "What ya doing?"

When I placed small bases on the floor, he'd kick his ball and run the bases. When I made my bed, he'd chase the wrinkles off the sheet with his beak. We had to watch him when we ate or he'd be right in the middle of our plate. He was such a part of the family that we left his cage door unlocked, and he went in and out as he pleased.

One day while Pretty Boy was on her shoulder, Mother forgot and went outside, and he flew away. When I got in from school, I knew something had happened because Pretty Boy's cage was on the front porch with the door open. I cried and cried.

We ran an ad in the paper: "Lost: Blue parakeet named Pretty Boy," with our phone number. Later that night, we got a call. It seems that a little boy all the way across town had been playing in his front yard, and Pretty Boy had landed on his shoulder.

They had a cage from owning a parakeet previously. That night while they were eating supper, they were reading the paper and saw our ad. When the parakeet started saying "My name is Pretty Boy. What's yours?" they called us, and we got him back. ❖

Growing Up With a Billy Goat

By Patricia Happel Cornwell

*I*t was supposed to be a joke. Uncle Dubby and his friend had driven all the way out to the farm at twilight, just a night or two after we had moved to the glorious, green country. There was a glint of mischief in my uncle's blue eyes. "I've got a surprise for you," he grinned. It was the hot, dry summer of 1951 when we moved from the growing city of Louisville, Ky., to the 100-year-old farmhouse with no indoor bathroom on 23 acres of hilly Indiana land. I was 7 and my brother was 10, and we thought farm life was wonderful from the first moment. We had never seen so much green, and the previous owners had left us an old tomcat named Tom. And we each had our own room. What more did we need?

Uncle Dubby and his friend were our very first visitors. My brother and I had run into the house, shrieking, "Someone's coming down the driveway!" Dad had come down with a bad case of flu and was so sick that evening that he couldn't get out of bed. We ushered my dainty mom out to meet the company.

"Since you all are farmers now, we thought the place wouldn't be complete without one of these," Uncle Dubby said. He opened the tailgate of the truck and out leaped the joke—the goat. He was a baby with the snowy-white, smooth coat of an Angora and the nubby beginnings of horns on his head. He brayed a silly, nervous utterance like the laugh of an embarrassed person. He looked at us and shook his head. We, too, looked at one another and shook our heads.

The adults were laughing and talking, but my brother and I were captivated by the awkward little animal. We stroked his back gingerly as he stood stoically, not moving his head, but *sliding* his eyes back to watch us. "Look at his eyes! They're square!" We were amazed at the goat's eyes, gray with yellow rectangles, centered with black.

"Can we really keep him?" my brother and I asked in disbelief.

"He's yours. We brought him all the way from Bowling Green." Mother raised her eyebrows, which meant, "We'll see."

Our prankster uncle never thought we'd keep the "crazy goat," but we did. We tied a wide blue ribbon in a bow around his neck and proudly showed him to neighbors and relatives.

No one else on our road had one. He was a "deodorized" billy, we were told. Unlike "unde-odorized" billies, he always smelled like talcum powder. We named him Billy, which, in his adulthood was elevated to The William Goat, and in his old age to Old Bill.

Billy grew fat-bellied and sleek. His horns were a marvel; they curved like a mountain goat's so that the sharp points aimed outward. Billy was proud of his horns. He shook them at us when we teased him, and he butted us hard, but carefully, in the thigh when he was really annoyed. Occasionally, he frightened us with a show of force, leaping into the air and coming down with his head tucked tight against his chest as if to inflict mortal injury. We were reminded that he could indeed hurt us if sufficiently provoked; yet, Billy was a playmate.

We loved to spoil Billy with treat. He learned to prance on his back feet to win an ear of corn. We tested his supposed goat's appe-tite for tin cans, but he never cared for them. He preferred bologna sandwiches with plenty of mustard, and he ate poison ivy as if it were candy. He also loved the taste of cigarettes and had an unfortunate yen for all varieties of gar-den vegetables.

Bill was a specialist at cleaning out a fence line. In summer, Daddy would "stake him out" on a chain next to the fence and move him so many feet each day. Our job was to keep Billy's chain untangled. He would walk one direction around the stake until he was wound up tight, his head to the ground, bleating pitifully. He never understood that moving in the opposite direction would free him. It was also our job to see that he had plenty of water and a good chunk of red mineral salt.

Billy's summer employment was to eat the poison ivy and wild roses from between the wires of the mesh fence. Businesslike, he nibbled swiftly, as if in a furious hurry, deftly stripping the leaves from the rose briars and capturing the ivy vines between his rubbery lips. During his poison ivy duty, we were admon-ished not to hug or pet him. His blithe resistance to the dreaded itch was one more reason we kids thought him an admirable animal.

At Halloween, we had to make sure that Billy was not stationed too near the road. Teen-age boys not acquainted with a goat were apt to think he was some kind of living, breathing joke. Although he had *come* to us as a joke, he was now a beloved member of our extended farm family, but being a fighter by nature, Billy invited confrontations with strangers.

One confrontation I'll never forget: I heard my mother huffing in her exasperated way, muttering under her breath. For once, she was not sure how to proceed.

"What's wrong?" I asked.

Our prankster uncle never thought we'd keep the "crazy goat," but we did.

"That crazy goat! He's got his horns caught in the sleeves of your daddy's best shirt!" There stood Old Bill, captured by the shirt he had attacked as it billowed in the breeze on the clothesline. He loved wash day and would come up into the yard to chew the buttons off the clothes on the line. He especially loved shirt fights, but he had lost this one.

Mom was afraid he would rip Dad's good white shirt with the French cuffs, but she was equally afraid to take hold of the cantankerous animal to free him. With broom in hand, she ventured out. Together we managed to separate goat and shirt. Billy shook his head in disgust and pranced away in great dignity.

"It's a good thing," my mother said bravely afterward, discovering the shirt was unharmed.

One time we had to move away from the farm when my father was transferred in his job. Daddy sadly walked Billy down the road to leave him with a neighbor. We closed up the old house but did not sell it.

The new house was fancy and the new job a promotion, but our father yearned for the farm. Six months later, we were back. The first thing Dad did the day we got back was go down to the neighbor's and bring home our goat.

The funniest thing Billy ever did still makes me smile. During the summer, we hung a heavy canvas hammock between two of the immense maples in our back yard. Anyone who took a notion could climb into the hammock and have a heavenly nap, rocked by a gentle breeze and sung to sleep by chirping birds.

One day we spied Billy eyeing the hammock. It swung lazily in the breeze, and he seemed to sway as it swayed. Suddenly he put a forefoot on it and stood, balancing on his remaining three feet, swaying with the rhythm of the hammock until it ceased to rock violently. Up went the other forefoot. Again he waited, swaying until the rocking slowed.

Finally, Billy hitched one back leg up, then the other, and rolled over into the hammock. He lay there all afternoon, rocking himself in the hammock the way a child throws his weight forward and backward in a swing.

We had a whole herd of baby-faced Hereford cattle, and Billy became their self-appointed mascot. He left them only for occasional trips into Dad's garden or Mom's flowers or for a solitary nap in the hammock. The old farmers in the vicinity had told Dad that cows would never get diseases as long as a goat stays with the herd. It sounded like an old farmer's tale, but in all the years Billy chaperoned the herd, we never had a sick cow.

Billy got cranky when he got older. He became impatient with the big, dopey cows, and one day he jabbed a horn into the side of gentle, pregnant Buttercup, the matriarch of the herd and our favorite. Buttercup was unhurt, but Dad was angry. Billy was banished from the pasture.

Both my brother and I were grown and married before Old Bill died of old age when he was 15. Dad buried him on a slope of the old apple orchard back near the creek and put a stone marker on the spot.

Having seen cats, dogs, pigs, chickens, rabbits, steers and heifers come and go, we took comfort in the longevity of old Billy, the goat we grew up with. We fed and watered him, protected him, petted him, teased him, tugged the winter mat of fur from him each spring and even hugged and kissed him when our mother wasn't looking. He came to us as a joke, but it was a long, happy joke with a good punch line. ❖

Hope

By Anita Norris Olson

Hope was a little white Nubian goat with long, floppy ears. She lived with her mother in a barn and corral on a far corner of property owned by Bob and Francis Bradbury, friends of my mother who had kennels and raised Scottish terriers.

During the 1940s, I spent summers and other school holidays with the Bradburys. They had acquired the goats because they felt that goat's milk was more easily digested by both dogs and humans. I adored all the dogs and helping out with the kennels.

Hope became my cherished pet. Each morning, she bleated at the corral gate, anticipating my visit. She followed me everywhere, and she stayed with me until I put her back in her corral. Often I was sent to the little country store that was a short walk away through dense woods. Hope always went with me, and at these times, I put a rope around her neck so that I could tether her to the post outside the store while I was inside.

One especially hot afternoon on the way home, we stopped in the woods to rest in the shade. I sat down beside an old log and watched Hope nibbling at the end of her rope. I was tired from a morning of kennel duties and fell asleep.

When I awoke, I was startled to find the rope gone pulled out of my hand, and Hope was not in sight. I feared she had wandered off. Needless to say, I was very happy when I spotted her in the dappled shade, munching around.

Hope was such an intelligent, comical little animal. She actually played hide-and-seek with me, and loved to eat the prunes that I fed her from the prune tree that grew near her corral. She always spit out the pits.

Seventy years have sped by since those days, and I still often thought of Hope. She became one of my most cherished and happiest memories. ❖

Floyd's Goat

By Herb T. M. Kliethermes

Some people in our neighborhood had dogs for pets and some had cats, but Floyd had a billy goat, complete with 5-inch horns. Floyd kept Billy in his back yard, which was surrounded by a 5-foot fence. Billy was tame and well fed, so he had no inclination to venture beyond the yard.

Floyd and I had seen a movie about a boy in a foreign country who delivered cans of milk in a cart pulled by a goat. We thought that was a great idea. We could build a cart and fashion a harness. Then Billy could pull us around. We would be the envy of every kid in the neighborhood.

During the Depression, funds were tight in every household, and there certainly weren't any available for such a frivolous project as a goat cart. So we scrounged up materials as best we could. Floyd's mom gave us an old clothesline. My mom gave us a couple of broken belts, and we found some old shoestrings.

We had everything for the harness; now for the cart. Between two rusty, broken wagons, we were able to salvage four wheels. We got some produce crates from behind the grocery store and some lumber from an abandoned shed. Great! We had all the necessary materials. With the precision and skill of two 12-year-old boys, we fashioned a harness for Billy and built a cart.

The big day came for the test run. While making the harness, we had put the straps and ropes around Billy several times to check the fit, so getting the harness on him was no problem. Floyd and I debated as to who should drive for the trial run. We flipped a coin and I won. I sat in the cart, ready to go.

In the movie we had seen, the boy had encouraged the goat to move forward by tapping him on the rump with a stick; a second tap and the goat would stop. But evidently, Billy had not seen that movie, because he did not respond accordingly. He didn't budge despite the taps. I tried "Giddy-yap!" a few times, but that didn't work either.

House of White Birches nostalgia archives

We were in a quandary as to what would motivate Billy. I thought that perhaps because of his thick hide, he wasn't feeling the taps on his rump. So I tried something a little stronger—a good whack.

Boy! Did *that* ever motivate him! Billy took off like a horse from a starting gate. He bolted across the yard and took one giant leap over the fence. He cleared the fence just fine—but I flew through the air and landed on the ground, and our carefully engineered cart and harness were left hanging on the fence in a shambles.

We gained a healthy respect for Floyd's goat, Billy, that day. My cuts and bruises healed, and we never tried to conform Billy to our way of thinking again. ❖

Gram's Georgie Boy

By J.B. O'Reilly

How my Gram ever had the forbearance to have Georgie in the house, I'll never know. Of course, she only had one child—Mama, known by her nickname, Gerry. Gerry was short for Geraldine, of which Mama wasn't terribly fond. So I figured that with only one child, this must have given Gram more room for patience with the four-legged creatures allowed in the house. From what I've been told, animals like Georgie were as clean or cleaner than a lot of house pets.

Since Gram had lived in town most of her life, she had never been surrounded by hundreds of these critters at one time. I, on the other hand, had. Oh, did I neglect to mention that Georgie was a member of the Yorkshire family? He had been the runt of the litter.

That's how Gram came to have this "special" white piglet. In fact, Georgie was only one of many she'd raised. Runts usually didn't make it if they stayed in the litter.

Did I mention that Georgie was a member of the Yorkshire family?

When they were small, she fed them with baby bottles, just like human babies. Behind the wood-burning cookstove in her kitchen, Gram kept a small wooden crate fitted with an old flannel sheet for just this purpose.

When the runts were big enough to withstand the change, she usually put them in a pen outside by the woodshed. Somehow, though, Georgie had a hard time accepting the fact he was anything but human. He would not give up the security of the house. This was going to complicate things just a little bit.

The Springer family who lived on a farm south of town gave the runts to Gram. Gram always appreciated these thoughtful gifts. Sometimes she had two or three at one time. Gram would raise them, mainly on scraps, until they were around 200–225 pounds. Then they would go to the butcher. This gave her and Grandpa Frank and Mama some much-needed meat in their diets.

The hams and bacon were smoked, and Gram usually canned the rest of the meat. This was the only means they had to preserve much of their food, as they didn't have a freezer.

Yes, Gram was very thankful for these runts, for her only means of making a living was doing washings for others.

Grandpa Frank couldn't work much. He had worked at the elevator for many years, but when he developed a cancerous growth on the side of his face, it made working regularly nearly impossible. He ended up working on some bridge construction when he had enough strength.

This really affected their income, so the pigs were a much-needed blessing. Thank goodness for a large garden that produced bountifully and gave them vegetables as well.

It was also a blessing that Georgie wasn't the only runt Gram raised that year. Those scraps had done their job. Even though he grew into a rather large and impressive hog, he continued to think he was still a little piglet.

Needless to say, Georgie had captured a special place in Gram's heart. He politely followed her wherever she went, in the house or outside.

He would constantly *oink* away, and Gram would chatter right back at him. You'd think they were having an in-depth conversation.

There was one particular moment Mama talked about repeatedly. Gram had just brought in the freshly washed bedclothes and had gone directly upstairs to put them back on the beds. Georgie had been following her around all day, as usual.

This time, though, she had slipped away from him somehow. He must have been otherwise occupied. He hadn't noticed that Gram had come into the house.

When he finally realized she wasn't with him, he came to the front door and stood outside, insistently oinking and squealing, trying to get someone's attention.

When this failed to get the desired results, he started nosing the screen door until it opened enough for him to get his snout between it and the door frame. That was all he needed. In no time, he was through the door and in the house.

He scurried to the kitchen first. Not finding Gram there, he made a beeline for the living room. There he found Mama reading. With an *oink, oink, oink,* he nudged Mama as if to ask, "Where's my lady?"

Mama shrugged and replied, "Don't know, Georgie. She might be upstairs." About that same moment, they both heard Gram walking around in Mama's bedroom just above them.

Yep! She surely was upstairs. Georgie quickly ran to the bottom of the stairs. *Oink! Oink! Oink!* he loudly squealed as he stepped up on the first stair with his front legs.

Gram called out to him that she would be right down, but Georgie only knew he heard her voice, and he interpreted that as an invitation to come up. I imagine that was quite a sight, seeing this rather large hog working his way up the stairs.

"I'll be right down, Georgie," said Gram as she came out of Mama's room. She couldn't believe her eyes when she saw who was coming up those stairs toward her. He wanted to be wherever she was, and nothing was going to stop him!

"Well now, Georgie Boy, just how are we going to get you back *down* these stairs?" remarked Gram. In response, he let loose with a long string of happy oinks.

"Oh, Georgie, you are impossible!" she said, chuckling. Good old Georgie—he'd follow her anywhere, even back down those steps. This charismatic pig was going to be a difficult one to butcher when the time came. It probably was going to be nigh unto an impossible task.

Yes, he was the cleanest, whitest Yorkshire pig, and he had won Gram's heart in an incredible way. He was a character, an unusual, unforgettable pet—Gram's Georgie Boy. ❖

Photograph copyright © 2008, www.stockxpert.com

Ethel

By Ann Givens

One summer, my husband, George, bought 10 very young turkeys from a neighbor to fatten up and put in the freezer. Our daughter, Christina, was an avid animal lover, and she fell in love with one of the turkeys.

This turkey was friendlier than the other nine. She would eat out of your hand, then stand as tall as she could to look up at you and beg for more. She was not afraid of us from day one.

Christina named the turkey Ethel, even though we told her that when they were all big enough, they would be butchered. But by the time the turkeys were fat enough to butcher, Christina and Ethel had become friends. George killed all the turkeys except Ethel because Christina cried and pleaded for her life.

Now, in the pen where we kept the turkeys, there were also five or six hens, a rooster and two ducks. After the turkeys had been killed, one of the ducks died. The one that was left was lonely and started following Ethel around.

Ethel put up with the duck, Herman, always on her tail—most of the time, that is. But being a temperamental turkey, every once in a while, Ethel would turn on Herman and flog him good.

In the fall, when the flowerbeds were no longer in bloom and couldn't be ruined by chickens fluffing in the loose dirt, we would turn them all into the yard and let them come and go as they pleased. What a sight: Ethel, a huge turkey, waddling across the yard with Herman adoringly waddling along behind. We never saw one without the other. At night, Ethel slept in the corner of the chicken pen with Herman by her side.

Ethel still flogged Herman, but not as often. They became inseparable. When Herman went for a swim in a little pond in our neighbor's pasture, Ethel waited on the bank until he tired of it. Then both would waddle back to the yard, Ethel always in the lead.

One day when Christina and I returned from an errand in town, we discovered that a dog had killed Herman. Ethel was quietly lying by his side. She had somehow escaped harm. For a long time after that, Ethel wandered about aimlessly. She seemed lost without her pal.

Finally, Ethel turned to people to ease her loneliness. She was an aggressive turkey, and thought everyone loved her as Herman had. She loved to be petted on her head; in fact, she insisted on it. Of course, people who didn't know her like we did thought she was a pest and tried to shoo her away. But this always upset Ethel. She would back off, fluff up her feathers, spread her wings and run at them viciously. By this time, one of us would usually see what was happening and call to her and pet her, explaining our unique bird to the visitors.

> *Ethel loved to be petted on her head; in fact, she insisted on it.*

When we petted Ethel on her little head, she would let her neck go limber, lean toward us and close her eyes—what a sight! Soon she would be satisfied and take her leave to do her own thing, such as bully the chickens away from the feeder, or scatter them if they were picking at something on the ground.

Christina eventually grew old enough to date. If she failed to tell her date about the unique creature we let run loose in our yard, or failed to meet him at the door, Ethel would run up to him, wanting to be loved. Usually the boys didn't pay much attention to her, and this upset Ethel no end. A few of the boys ran back to their cars with Ethel on their heels.

Ethel lived to be 7 years old. She was a loving pet and a conversation piece around our house. We missed her very much after she died. She was a very special and loving friend.

We still look for a personality like hers when we are around turkeys. But, like people, there are no two alike. ❖

The Naked Canary

By Joyce Normandin

*I*n her 37th year, in 1945, after 16 years of marriage, my Aunt Anne fell totally and completely in love. The object of her affection was a small yellow canary. She had visited a new neighbor with a cherry cobbler as a welcome gift. Invited inside, she heard chirping and singing and spied a bird cage with a canary. She asked the neighbor about it and was informed that it was a special canary, a guaranteed singer.

Aunt Anne came home in ecstasy, her feet barely touching the ground. She made a special dinner, and when her husband, my Uncle Ed, was drinking his coffee and polishing off his second piece of cake, she brought up the subject of the neighbor's canary.

Now, Uncle Ed was of the mind that the children had enough pets. There was a St. Bernard, which galumphed around the house and yard, chewing bones and shoes indiscriminately, and a tabby cat who spent his days stalking mice, moles and birds in the back yard or snoozing complacently in a big, overstuffed chair near the fireplace. A large bowl of goldfish endlessly circled their confines. A hamster nibbled his way through meals and treats.

"But this wouldn't be for the children, but my very own pet, just for me," she sighed, "and it would sing and cheer me all day." Aunt Anne pleaded, "Next week is my birthday, and I can't think of anything I would want more." Uncle Ed said that he would take her to the pet store the following weekend.

The next Saturday, dressed in her best blue hat and dress, Aunt Anne and Uncle Ed set out to purchase a canary. Aunt Anne strolled back and forth along the display of cages. Finally she selected a sweet little canary that was a guaranteed singer. They piled a cage, a cage stand, birdseed, and other assorted paraphernalia into the car. Aunt Anne sat with the bird in a box on her lap.

Arriving home, she had to decide where to set up the cage. She pondered and finally opted for the dining room window, a rather large one, which captured some of the morning sun.

The canary, now named Chaucer, thrived. It was just about everything Aunt Anne had dreamed … except for one thing: It never sang!

Aunt Anne was not one to give up. She talked to it,

played music for it and tinkled on the piano, but the canary never made so much as a peep.

After a few months, she called the pet store. They told her that their birds were guaranteed to sing, and if she brought it back, they would be glad to exchange it for another bird. However, by now, Aunt Anne had bonded with little Chaucer. "It would be like giving up my own child," she declared. And so, Chaucer became a permanent, if silent, family member.

Time marches on, as they say, and Chaucer remained Aunt Anne's beloved, if quiet, pet, and she adored him. No one dared mention his "infirmity."

Then, one summer, the family had an opportunity to spend a month in Cape Cod. They could take Butch, the dog. The cat by now had passed to the great sandbox in the sky. The hamster would be taken by a cousin, along with the goldfish.

That left Chaucer. A 7- or 8-hour road trip in a car without air conditioning was just not doable. Aunt Anne cited Chaucer's delicate constitution. "I'll be glad to mind him for you," volunteered Aunt Marian. And so, Chaucer went with her, to take up temporary residence in her living room window.

Following instructions carefully, Aunt Marian fed, watered, changed cage paper and talked to him. She played music for him or stood by his cage humming. Unfortunately, Chaucer did not respond well. He seemed depressed. Aunt Marian moved the cage about the house trying to find, as she put it, "the happiest spot." She began to notice some feathers in the bottom of the cage. *Oh,* she thought, *he is probably molding.* She meant *molting.*

She increased his food and moved Chaucer to the kitchen window, but more and more feathers appeared. She sang to him more often and even began to move Chaucer to her bedroom at night so he would not be lonely, but Chaucer lost more and more feathers.

By the end of the third week, almost all that remained on the bird were little tufts of yellow fuzz. Aunt Marian was frantic. She

could not take it to the vet, she reasoned, as she was afraid that it would catch cold since it had no "clothes" on. So she called the vet, and a diet change was recommended—alas, to no avail!

By now, although the situation seemed dire, the one most affected was Aunt Marian. Chaucer, in a sudden change of attitude, merrily fluttered about in his cage. He had awoken from his depression with a new vitality.

Then, believe it or not, one day, Chaucer began to sing! Never in all its years had it so much as let loose with a single note. Now it had become a Caruso of canaries! It sang in the morning, it sang in the afternoon, it sang in the evening. The only way to turn the thing off was to cover the cage.

Aunt Marian uncovered the cage to reveal the naked canary. Aunt Anne screamed and almost fainted.

When Aunt Anne arrived home from vacation, her first stop was at Aunt Marian's to pick up her canary. "Now, don't get excited," Aunt Marian said to her. "Just take a seat and I will explain."

"Oh, my heavens!" Aunt Anne exclaimed, "Chaucer is dead!"

"Oh, no," Aunt Marian assured her, "it's just that he looks just a little bit different." Aunt Marian slowly uncovered the cage to reveal the naked canary. Aunt Anne screamed and almost fainted.

Then suddenly, almost on cue, Chaucer began to sing his little canary heart out. His wee vocal chords belted out one note after another. Aunt Anne could hardly believe her ears. Chaucer! Singing! The silent bird of years past had been transformed into a virtuoso! His repertoire seemed endless and spectacular.

Aunt Anne cried with happiness. She hugged Aunt Marian and forgave her. She took Chaucer home, resolved to love him despite his lack of feathers. Just hearing him sing was wonderful enough.

In the following weeks, Chaucer slowly began to grow feathers again. He lived a long and happy musical life, warbling his sweet songs all day to Aunt Anne's great joy—and Aunt Marian's great relief. ❖

Wayne's Bodyguard

By Iris Thompson

When my brother Wayne was a lad, he thought he would like to raise geese. He talked Dad into buying a pair at a farm auction. The goose proved to be a neglectful mother. She wouldn't sit on the eggs she laid, so Wayne spirited away the next batch of three as soon as they were laid and put them under a setting hen to hatch.

One egg produced a gosling. Wayne raised it in a large box in the house to protect it from the unpredictable spring weather. He took good care of the little creature, feeding and watering it and changing

1935 *Country Home*, House of White Birches nostalgia archives

the paper in the bottom of its cage. Since my brother was uncertain of his young charge's gender, he gave it a generic name: Goosie Duck.

The bird was just old enough to begin exchanging down for feathers when it also began to resent Wayne's intrusion into its territory. It displayed its displeasure by pinching Wayne with its tiny beak and flogging him with its wings.

Wayne gently retaliated by batting back. As the bird grew, so did the intensity of their battles. Wayne was forced to don a heavy coat and glove when tending his charge.

With age, the goose's gender became apparent. She was an ill-tempered goose. In spring, Goosie Duck was allowed to run free in the inner yard. The pair continued sparring in the evenings when it came time to put the goose back in the house.

Wayne was obliged to add heavy jeans and high boots to his protective clothing. Anyone else entering or leaving the yard gave Goosie Duck a wide berth or suffered the consequences.

Gradually the relationship between my brother and his goose changed. She started rubbing her head and body against his leg like a cat, and instead of shrieking and hissing, she began crooning softly. Wayne, in turn, gently stroked her head and body. From then on, they were constant companions except at night.

But she waited outside the back door for Wayne to come out each morning. So faithful was she in her vigil that it became necessary for Wayne to build a little house near the back door to protect her from inclement weather.

On occasion, Mom allowed Wayne to bring Goosie Duck into the house at lunch. His bodyguard sat under the table, close to his feet. The rest of us took care to keep our feet near our chairs. We got pinched if they strayed too close.

Wayne soon learned to use her protective nature to his advantage. He taunted and teased our older, bigger brother, Val, without fear of retribution. All he had to do was make a fuss like he was being hurt, and Goosie Duck would attack any assailant, including Val.

The goose followed Wayne everywhere around the farm. In her determination not to be separated from him, she often walked a quarter

of a mile to the next farm where the boys loaded hay onto the truck to bring home to the cattle.

They usually had the truck loaded by the time Goosie Duck reached her destination beside Wayne. Val would not allow her in the cab of the truck, so Wayne would give her a ride home on top of the load of hay.

When school started in the fall, Goosie Duck attempted to follow Wayne's school bus, but she had to return home when she lost sight of it. Then she moped around the barnyard all day, head hanging, and making a terribly sad, mournful sound.

Soon, however, she learned that the same bus that took her pal away in the mornings came over the hill south of the house in the evenings to deposit him at the end of the long lane. At the first sight of the bus, Goosie Duck stretched out her long neck and began to scream her elation.

Wayne soon learned to use her protective nature to his advantage.

Her wings were not strong enough to allow her to fly down the lane, but she was able to flap them hard enough so that she could skim along with the tips of her webbed feet barely touching the ground.

When she reached him, Wayne laid his books aside to take her in his arms. She nibbled him gently all over his face, neck and ears, crooning softly. This behavior astounded the bus driver and the children on the bus.

But Goosie Duck became a fickle little hussy the day she discovered her own reflection in the shiny bumper of the pickup. There were no more mournful sounds to be heard; instead, she rubbed her cheek against the image in the bumper. "They" nibbled softly, beak-to-beak, as she crooned to her new love. But as soon as the bus topped the hill, she forgot all about her new love as she rushed into Wayne's arms once more.

We all missed our feathered friend when the time came for her to leave us.

Wayne summed up his feelings for his feathered bodyguard when he said, "If animals go to heaven, surely Goosie Duck is there. Perhaps in some shiny, reflective corner, she will find her other love, who will keep her company until God's bus brings me over that last hill to join her once more." ❖

SPRINGTIME

Hare-Raising Times

By Kathleen W. Stobbe

There was a time when building codes and restrictions were much less stringent than they are today. But as populations increased and people lived closer together, cities and townships have been forced to pass much stricter laws to protect their citizens. Living in the country somewhat removed from the city, we were allowed certain privileges of animal ownership that made our lives more interesting and rewarding … or so it seems as I think back to the simpler way of life when I was a child.

Some of our neighbors kept a horse or two. Many of us learned to ride while still quite young. Chickens were common. Ducks paddled across ponds if there was one on the owner's land.

We were also allowed to fish in these ponds, and early on, we learned the various species of fish. Mostly we caught pan-size perch, but sometimes, a catfish or bass dangled from our worm-baited hook. Guernsey cows could be seen peacefully grazing in several fenced areas.

A friend, Raymond, had a parrot that screeched quite audibly, "Get otta here, ah'm desson." Another phrase he had was "No crackers, ple-e-ease." Raymond's parents were quick to tell everyone, "Our parrot had a previous owner."

Of course, the usual assortment of friendly dogs and purring cats abounded.

Our neighbors, Moss Murphy and his family, doted on rabbits.

Our neighbors, Moss Murphy and his family, doted on rabbits. Rabbits of every size and color could be seen bunny-hopping all over their hutches and Rabbit Acres, as the Murphy place was called. During daylight, they romped freely in a large, fenced-in area.

Occasionally, a little cottontail would escape, but everyone knew where he belonged, and Mr. Murphy soon had his adventurous rabbit safely back home. Sometimes the bunnies managed to invade Mrs. Murphy's vegetable garden. Anyone who retrieved one from the garden or returned one who'd wandered from home territory was rewarded with a nickel for his efforts and a grateful thank-you from the Murphys.

Most of the children in our neighborhood, me included, didn't realize that the rabbits were being raised to be table delicacies. I'd heard about "rabbit stew," but I never associated it with the cuddly bunnies I loved. I suppose that adults in our community thought it wise to conceal certain facts until children were old enough to comprehend such matters.

I did know that the Murphys loved their rabbits and kept their hutches and living area whistle clean. There were always pellets, greens and fresh water available. They named many of them after Irish cities and patted a busy little bunny's head when one came within reach.

Mr. Murphy spent many winter hours in his workshop, sawing and sanding pieces that would eventually became a small, wooden, rabbit-drawn cart. His wife, Martha, expertly painted each pull toy in soft, pastel colors.

These were given to family and neighbor children at Easter. Also, J.M. Jones Hardware in the town square sold the carts for a nominal price—*very* nominal considering the time and effort that went into their making. I wish I'd had the foresight to save at least one of the carts that I was lucky enough to receive as a gift.

During one very severe winter week in the '30s, Mr. Murphy moved the rabbits into the barn to shelter them from the cold. He decided to sleep in the barn to protect his furry friends from predators that sometimes invaded the area.

During his sleep, he was awakened by the soft nuzzling of fur on his face. One of the rabbits was alerting Mr. Murphy to trouble. In the glare of his flashlight, Mr. Murphy caught sight of a fox scooting out of the barn. All of the rabbits were spared because of the alertness of one. The weather soon moderated and the rabbits were back in their familiar, safe hutches at night.

"It's a good thing that Limerick, our rabbit, wakened Moss," Mrs. Murphy said later. "He sleeps so sound that he wouldn't have known if a tornado had passed through town."

The summer that I was 9 years old, Mrs. Murphy called and asked, "Would you like to come over and pick up your birthday gift?"

The box that they handed me held a cuddly, black-and-white baby rabbit. They had thoughtfully received permission from my parents for me to have one as a pet. I named him Murph.

Murph was a part of our family for many happy years. My dad had already made him a large hutch in anticipation of his arrival.

Living amid this farmlike atmosphere, we children learned to care for and respect animals and know their important role in our lives. Eventually, however, zoning laws took effect, and we could no longer keep livestock or fowl so close to the growing population.

But I never wonder why zoos are so popular with the young—and the young at heart. ❖

Lucky Ducky

By Geri Gladden

I was 6 years old in 1952 when my mother and father took me to the Monrovia Days carnival. Our town, Monrovia, Calif., hosts Monrovia Days each year. The celebration includes a big parade and carnival to commemorate the town's birthday in 1886. The carnival was always at the park in the middle of town.

My mother's boss was tending one of the booths that were giving away ducks as prizes. You had to throw a dime into a glass dish to win, and believe me, I don't know how I did it—or even if I *did* do it—but I won a beautiful little yellow baby duck. I was very excited, as were my parents.

We took the little duck home where we lived with my grandparents. Everyone loved Lucky, as I named that little duck. She was one of the smartest pets I ever had, and I'll tell you, I've had plenty of pets in my years.

She laid large eggs, which my grandmother used for baking. Most of all, she was my grandfather's little pet, as she spent a lot of time with him. As a result, the little duck grew to be bilingual. My grandparents were immigrants from Mexico and didn't speak much English. My grandfather would speak to Lucky in Spanish, and I would play with her and speak to her in English.

We also had a springer spaniel by the name of King. King was always leaving the yard, and Grandfather was always out looking for him. Grandfather and Lucky would go up and down the alley, looking for King. Speaking in Spanish, my grandfather would say to Lucky, "Go get that dog and bring him to me!" Then Lucky would start quacking and looking for King. When she found him, she would bring him to my grandfather by pecking him on the back of his legs until she got him all the way home.

Grandfather and Lucky are gone now, but I still have happy memories of them both. ❖

Our Little Girl

By Anna Barker Loudermilk

There was a time in the 1950s when one could order things from the Sears Roebuck catalog that you will not find on catalog pages today. Among these things were animals. One day, while browsing through its pages, Mama spied a picture of a little, long-eared animal. "Watson, pick up the phone and call Sears and Roebuck and order this burro. I want it for the grandchildren." And that is how Nina—meaning "little girl" in Spanish—came to live with us.

The day finally came for the burro to arrive. Dad and Talmage, my husband, had already put high sideboards on the back of Dad's GMC truck. They wanted a safe place for the little burro to ride.

Nina arrived in Statesville, N.C., a town about 12 miles from our home in the country. Wearing a rope halter, she was waiting at the railroad station when Dad and Talmage arrived.

Nina was much smaller than we expected; in fact, she appeared to have been just weaned. Dad was shocked. She was too little to ride in the back of the truck as they planned, so they brought her home in the cab, sitting between Dad and Talmage.

Soon after she arrived, I tried to get Nina down to the pasture gate on our farm. But she must have been tired and sore from the long train trip from Mexico, for she wouldn't budge.

In a surly mood, she decided she had had enough, and she sat down—*plop!*—right in the driveway, her legs sticking out in front of her. Finally, after much pulling, tugging and pleading, I got her to the gate and into the pasture.

There was plenty of grass and feed, and Nina began to grow. Of course, we loved her, and she was spoiled. She loved attention. Once when I

My son, David, on Nina, 1956.

was taking care of the cows, I leaned over a barrel to get some feed, and Nina slipped up behind me and pinched me on the backside. And she seemed to delight in slipping up behind a cow and grabbing a sample of milk.

Mama and Dad had a big pasture, too, so Nina spent part of the time at their farm and part of the time at ours. She lived with the cows at our farm; at Mama's, she shared the pasture with whatever was there at the time. Over the years, her neighbors there included cows, calves, chickens, hogs and even goats.

When Nina got old enough to ride, Mama bought a saddle. My son David and my sister's children, Tommy, Chris and Greg, enjoyed riding and playing with Nina. But they teased her, too. When Nina got tired of the boys, she just lay down and rolled. Whoever was on her back scrambled or fell off. Then they knew that Nina had had enough of their antics for the day.

While roaming around the pasture one day, Nina had a terrible accident. She stepped into a brush pile and her leg was broken. Frantic with worry, Mama called the veterinarian to come down and see if he could help her.

Mama was so afraid Nina would die. She went upstairs to her bedroom, praying that God would heal Nina's leg. They made a sling for Nina so that she could keep her weight off the broken leg. And it worked. God answered Mama's prayer, and Nina got well again.

Later, in the 1960s, my family and I moved away. Mama and Dad sold their farm, too, but before they moved, Nina went to live with someone else. One day, when I asked about Nina, I was told she had marched in the Fourth of July parade in Statesville. Wasn't that neat? ❖

My Little Friend

By Sallie L. Peeler

I grew up in North Carolina in the 1940s and 1950s. My dad passed away when I was 2 years old and my mama was pregnant with my little brother. So with four other children, she took us to live on my grandparents' farm. Even though the old farmhouse had no electricity or plumbing, our lives there were content and happy.

We got a lot of love from our mama and grandparents. My grandfather farmed, and Grandmother raised chickens for food and eggs. We had a huge garden from which everything was canned in jars for the cold winter months.

One spring, my grandmother was raising her usual chicks. She had a brood of bantam chicks. One chick was a runt. I took her for a pet and named her Pee Wee. I put a box on our back porch for her to sleep in. After awhile, she learned to fly up onto the rail that ran around our back porch.

Each morning when she heard me call her, there she'd be, waiting to be fed. I'd fill her water bowl and get feed from the sack of chicken feed my grandmother kept in our kitchen.

I must have been 7 or 8 years old. My little brother, who is two years younger, played with me. We did not have TV or the things children have today, so we spent our days exploring the woods around our house, playing in small creeks, catching minnows and tadpoles. Pee Wee watched us all the time.

We loved picking wild strawberries and blackberries. What wonderful pies those made! But little Pee Wee always got her fill first.

She was a wonderful and faithful pet. She was by my side wherever I went.

One morning she was not on her usual perch. She just sat on the porch. I called for my sister, who told me Pee Wee was very sick. I put her in her box. The next morning my beloved pet was gone. She had died during the night. My older brother buried her at the edge of our yard.

The old farmhouse has been gone for many years now. Now that I'm older, I understand how something as small and innocent as a little chicken could bring such joy to a small child. Those memories will remain for a lifetime. ❖

1958 *Rawleigh's Almanac and Cook Book,*
courtesy Janice Tate

The Brooklyn Rooster

Eileen Higgins Driscoll

I am a city girl from the Big Apple, New York City. My two sisters and I grew up during the Depression days of the 1930s. We lived in the bedroom community of Brooklyn. Reflecting back brings to mind large families, row houses, paved streets, subways, buses and trolleys. It was a neighborhood of friendly people, and most of them had children our age. It was a good place for children to grow up.

We always had a dog or a cat in our house, but one Easter Sunday, the bunny left a surprise for us along with the usual baskets of candy and pretty jelly beans. The Easter Bunny had left a little chicken for my brother! It was a tiny, fluffy, soft ball of yellow feathers. Two little black eyes peeked out over a tiny beak. It was the first time any of us had seen a real live chicken up close. He was a delight for us and our friends, too.

We took good care of him, and he quickly grew into a fine-looking rooster. He developed long feathers and a big red comb on top of his head. He never really got a proper name; we all just called him Chicken. But that seemed to suit him just fine because every time we called "Chicken!" he came to get another kernel of corn from our hand.

Dad fashioned a combination bed and rooster house for Chicken under the porch. Our back yard was his domain, and he seemed content.

Every morning at dawn, he would climb up on top of Dad's weather vane and, in his best voice, announce, "Cockle-do-di-do!" He was loud enough to wake the whole neighborhood.

One day, the Board of Health came to our door with a citation for keeping barnyard animals in the city. Someone had reported us. Chicken had to move. We all cried when Mother told us Chicken had moved to the country. The neighbor's kids cried with us. We missed our Chicken. He was such a good pet! ❖

George

By Linda Roll

When I was 9, my father came home from work one day with a big cardboard box. Inside the box was an adorable, half-grown yellow duckling. The duckling had been purchased by city people as an Easter gift to their children. They had nowhere to keep him as he grew, so they offered him to us.

Our house was in Rosedale, Pa., in the middle of a public playground, with a little creek running alongside it.

We named the duckling George and immediately took him down to the creek. He had *never* been in water, but he knew exactly what to do, and he absolutely loved it.

George became very attached to us. He followed us everywhere. We would tease him by hiding from him, and he would flap his wings and quack loudly as if calling us. He didn't want us out of his sight.

Dad made George a pen with a little ramp leading up to it. George went into it every night before dark. One morning, we found a big egg in the straw. My father thought someone was playing a trick on us. But as the days went by, another egg was produced each day. Every egg was a double-yolker, and Dad ate them every morning as part of his breakfast.

Turns out that George was a Georgette.

I loved her with all my heart. I'm touched deeply each year at the county fair, when I see the fuzzy little ducklings. It takes me right back to my Georgie. ❖

The Horse That Wouldn't Whoa

By Judy Goodspeed

I don't remember just when I first saw Tuffy, since horses came and went frequently at our place. My dad, Buck Goodspeed, was a professional roper and was well-known for his ability to train top-notch roping horses. When he wasn't traveling to rodeos, Dad trained horses and practiced roping every day at our arena across the creek from the barn. He almost never failed to get the results he sought from a horse, but Tuffy was one of the rare exceptions.

My older siblings, Janice and Sonny, were already in school when I was born, and since I had no one to play with, I became Dad's shadow. Each morning, Dad and I would head out to the barn. I helped him brush and saddle two or three horses, and then we would ride to the arena.

Tuffy, one of the horses Dad was training that year, was a beautiful chestnut-sorrel gelding. He stood about 16 hands tall and was very stout. Dad said he looked like a cross between a giraffe and an elephant.

Dad asked me if I would like to have the good-for-nothing horse.

He had the makings of a good steer horse, except that he wouldn't stop when Dad hollered "Whoa!"

Tuffy did everything else just as he was supposed to. He was calm in the box, he scored well, he caught steers quickly, and he turned away from the trip. But he wouldn't stop. Dad tried everything. He put a jerk line on him, but Tuffy kept on going. Then he logged him, but Tuffy still kept on going. It became a contest of wills, and Tuffy finally won.

One morning after another workout with Tuffy, Dad rode back to the chute and asked me if I would like to have the good-for-nothing horse. I flew off the chute like a flying squirrel! I assured Dad that I would be happy to own such a great horse and that I would take good care of him.

Having my own horse was a dream come true. I danced a little jig and held Tuffy tight. I'm sure I was the happiest girl in Oklahoma. Mother, however, was not so happy about Dad's gift. I was only 4 and Tuffy was very big. Dad told Mother that I would be fine if I didn't fall off. Mother quit complaining, but she confined me to the pasture near the house.

Now that I had Tuffy, I could relive all the Western movies I saw on the big screen. We tracked and apprehended outlaws, scouted for wagon trains and cavalry units, and hunted buffalo so my tribe could have food.

Cowboys drive stock into the corral at the Pie Town, N.M., rodeo in October 1940.

No cowboy, soldier or Indian could have had a more wonderful horse. The days weren't long enough. I never tired of riding, and Tuffy was as dependable as the sunrise.

For four wonderful years, Tuffy and I chased outlaws, rode with the cavalry, helped with cattle drives to and from summer pasture, and even peddled garden seed to the neighbors. Dad was winning enough ropings to provide a good living for our family, and life was good. Then, on July 8, 1951, our lives changed drastically.

Dad was to rope that day in a matched roping against Ike Rude at the Waynoka rodeo. On his first steer, Dad's horse became tangled in the rope and fell. Dad suffered a severe head injury.

After a lengthy hospital stay, he came home, but he was confined to bed for months. He could not leave the house for more than a year.

Dad had been our only means of support, so our financial condition became critical. The time came when it was necessary to sell some of our cattle and horses, and Tuffy was one of the horses that had to be sold. Although I knew my parents had no choice, I was crushed.

On the day of the sale, Dad asked if I wanted to ride Tuffy in the sale ring, and I told him that I would. As I rode into the ring, the auctioneer announced, "Tuffy. Ridden and owned by Judy Goodspeed." When the bidding stopped and Tuffy was sold, I dismounted and removed my saddle. Kind hands were there to help me.

I hugged my friend one last time, told him I would never forget him and walked out of the ring. Dad met me at the gate. I knew that he, too, was sick at heart.

My life became one of deep sadness. I was sad about losing Tuffy and sad to see my dad in terrible shape. He was improving, but slowly. I told myself that I was just glad that I had owned that old horse for as long as I had.

Time went by, and I discovered another love—books. I avoided people and stayed buried in a book as much as possible. Gradually my wound healed, Dad healed, and life began to get better again. Five years after his accident, Dad entered rodeo competition again. He placed in every major steer roping he entered, but he knew that seconds and thirds were not good enough. So he made the difficult decision to retire and he hung up his ropes.

As it turned out, my love of books eventually resulted in my becoming the first of my family to obtain a college degree. Perhaps if Tuffy and I had stayed together, I would have become an outlaw on the run or a scout on some frontier.

Whether outlaw or scout, I could have been sure of one thing: If I were to ride Tuffy wide open across the countryside and holler "Whoa," he would stop every time. You see, that is one of the secrets that Tuffy and I shared. ❖

Photograph by Russell Lee courtesy the FSA/OWI Collection, the Library of Congress

The Broken Promise

By Sylva Mularchyk

*S*ally had a beautiful shepherd-collie whose name was Rover. They went everywhere together. They went for long walks in the fields, and sometimes they wandered down the road toward the town where Sally's grandma lived. But they never walked all the way, because it was too far—at least 5 miles.

Sally had a new friend—a little black-and-white calf that her daddy had given her. She couldn't take the little calf for walks, but she played with it in the barnyard, and they had great fun running and tumbling in the straw.

There was something else that was new, too. Sally's mother had a new baby boy. She said it was Sally's little brother. He was very tiny—too small to play with, but Mother said he would grow very fast. About the only thing Sally could see that he did was to cry and then wet his diapers. One day a neighbor drove his truck into the yard and he got out to talk with Sally's daddy. He waved his hand toward the clothesline where a whole row of diapers was swinging in the breeze. "Your wife keeps busy, I see!" he laughed.

> *"Daddy! Daddy!" she screamed.*
> *That man is taking my calf away!"*

"Yes," Daddy nodded, "but the worst of it is that she has to scrub all of our clothes on that washboard."

The man leaned closer to Daddy. "I have an old washing machine at home. We don't need it since we got a new one. But I do need a calf. Now, since you have something I want and I have something you want, maybe we can make a trade."

Sally didn't hear any more as the two men walked toward the barn, but the next day, the man came again, and he brought the washing machine for Mother. Sally had to laugh when she saw how happy Mother was and how she kissed Daddy!

Then Daddy went outside, and a little later, Sally heard the sound of the truck starting. She went to the door and saw it just going out the gate. Suddenly she heard a faint little "Moooo!" coming from the back of the truck. It was her calf! What was it doing in the truck? She started to run after it, but she soon realized that she couldn't catch up, so she turned and ran to Daddy.

"Daddy! Daddy!" she screamed. "That man is taking my calf away!"

He looked down at Sally, and it seemed as if he remembered something he'd forgotten. His smile faded and he knelt by Sally while he patted Rover on the nose.

"Sally, I guess we forgot to tell you—but we traded your calf for Mother's washing machine."

"What's trading?"

"It means we have a washing machine and he has a new calf."

"It means I don't have a calf anymore," Sally said.

"Well, I guess it does," Daddy admitted.

"But you said it was *mine*—my very own! You promised me!" Tears began to roll down her cheeks.

He reached out to her, but she turned and ran with Rover behind her. "Sally! Where are you going?"

"I'm leaving! I'm going to live with Grandma!"

For a minute, Daddy didn't know what to say, but finally he called after her, "Well, I hope you'll come back and see us sometime!"

Sally was already a long way down the road toward Grandma's, and she slowed to a walk. She wished she had stopped long enough to get an apple to eat before she had started out, but she had been too angry with Daddy to think of that.

"I guess Grandma will be happy to see us, Rover," she lamented. "She always said she'd like to have us come and live with her."

Sally threw a stick, and Rover ran and picked it up and brought it back to her, but she soon tired of playing. The June sun seemed to grow hotter every minute. She looked back toward the farm. She could barely see it now because it was so far away.

The weeds growing along the road were so high, but she thought she could see Daddy standing in the yard, still watching her. She got a funny feeling in her tummy, like she wanted to go back, but she remembered that she was angry—and her little calf was gone.

She tried to walk a little faster toward town, her little white towhead bobbing along. At last Sally was really tired and hungry. She decided she had to sit and rest for a few minutes. She made a shady little nest beside a clump of bushes and Rover lay down beside her. She put her head on Rover's soft, furry neck, and before they knew it, they were both fast asleep.

That's the way Daddy found them. He picked Sally up tenderly and carried her back to the farm. She didn't wake up until she heard Mother say, "Well, Daddy, do you think you learned your lesson today?"

Daddy laughed. "I sure did. I've learned that I must keep promises I make. I'll have to get Sally a new pet."

There was another sound, too—it was the baby crying. So while they were all laughing and crying, Sally hugged Daddy a little tighter and murmured, "I wasn't going to stay very long at Grandma's house. I'm awfully glad to be home!"

This story is true. You see, I was that little girl named Sally. ❖

Our Pet Lamb

By O'Dell McDonald

The year was 1941. I was 11 years old. There were nine in our family—Mom, Dad, five boys and two girls. We lived on a doctor's farm in middle Tennessee. My dad and brothers took care of the farm. We had corn, fruit trees, hay and plenty of gardens. We had plenty of food for the summer, and my mom canned fruits and vegetables for the winter.

There was always plenty of work for all of us. There was wood to cut for the wood-burning cook-stove and four fireplaces. There were cows to milk, and chickens, horses, ponies, pigs and sheep to feed and take care of. Rain or shine, ice or snow, the work had to go on every day. We never got finished; we just had to stop when it got dark. There was no electricity, just coal-oil lamps and lanterns and the moon.

Yes, farm life was hard, and there was little payback in those days. But sometimes it was fun and full of surprises. One such surprise came one cold morning. Very early, our dad went to one of the barns to feed the sheep and see if any lambs had been born during the night. When he came home, shivering from the cold, he was carrying something in his arms: a wee baby lamb, cold and trembling, and so weak that we could hardly hear it *baa*.

We children were getting ready for school, and would have to walk two and a half miles to get there. But when we saw Dad come in with the lamb, we all ran to see and excitedly huddled around them at the warm fireplace.

Everyone wanted to hold it. But our dad said no. This baby lamb had been forsaken by her mom, who had given birth to twins. She refused to let this one nurse. I knew it would die if it didn't get food pretty soon.

We didn't have a baby bottle, but we found another bottle and cut a piece of hollow cane. We filled the bottle with good, warm, fresh cow's milk. Then we stuck the cane into the bottle like a straw, wrapped a cloth around it to hold it in tightly, and began feeding the lamb.

We named her Betsy. She grew up healthy and strong. We took good care of her. She'd run and play with us and the dogs. She was *always* glad when we got home from school so we could play. We had fun with her.

> *This lamb had been forsaken by her mom, who had given birth to twins.*

One day, my brothers said, "I think we'll go 'babbit' hunting." They got their guns and called the dogs. Betsy was watching and getting excited. Wherever they were going, she was getting ready to go too. They went through the gate, the dogs and old Betsy running and jumping. They climbed the hills and went across the fields, the dogs chasing rabbits and old Betsy running along with them. When they got back, they said she had enjoyed the hunt as much as the dogs had. We all got a big laugh out of that.

One day as she was running around and playing, she ran into the house and jumped up onto Mom's white bedspread. Mom saw her. "Oh, no you don't, little lady," she said. Then she said, "This lamb has got to go."

"Oh, Mom, don't be mad," we pleaded. "She's just a big pet!" I ran and petted her. She liked that and rubbed up against my dress.

One day the doctor told my dad, "I'm going to sell all the sheep." All of us hated to see her go—except Mom. She said, "I *told* you she'd have to go." But that was a sad day when we had to tell her goodbye.

We still think about her. We always wondered if she thought she was a dog. I guess we'll never know. ❖